Hoop Tales:

UConn Huskies
Women's Basketball

Hoop Tales™ Series

Hoop Tales:
UConn Huskies Women's Basketball

Terese Karmel

INSIDERS' GUIDE®

GUILFORD, CONNECTICUT
AN IMPRINT OF THE GLOBE PEQUOT PRESS

INSIDERS' GUIDE®

Text design: Casey Shain
Cover photos: *front cover:* Rebecca Lobo (UConn Division of Athletics);
back cover: top, Nykesha Sales (UConn Division of Athletics); bottom,
NCAA trophy (UConn Division of Athletics).

Library of Congress Cataloging-in-Publication Data is available.

ISBN 0-7627-3501-5

Manufactured in the United States of America
First Edition/First Printing

This book is dedicated to Naomi Ruth Karmel and Caroline Elizabeth Thomason, who already show the promise and qualities to be as fine as the women in this book.

Contents

Acknowledgments

A book of this scope is as much the result of others' hard work as my own. In this regard I would like to thank the following individuals and organizations for their contributions.

Several people at the University of Connecticut were generous with their time and material, in particular Randy Press and Mike Enright of the athletic communications department, and Mark Roy of the university communications office.

I would also like to thank the individuals and various publications that have supported me over the years in my endeavor to cover this team. They include Kevin Crosbie, publisher of the *Willimantic Chronicle*; Jim Smith, executive editor, and Bob Morrissette, sports editor, of the *Meriden Record-Journal*; and Charles Monagan, editor, of *Connecticut* magazine.

In addition, Ellen and Mike Urban and Julie Marsh, my editors on this project, are to be thanked for their sensitivity to the text.

My heartfelt appreciation goes to the members of my writers' group: Leslie Johnson, Wally Lamb, Pam Lewis, and Ellen Zahl. Over the years these talented individuals have provided me with a climate of support and encouragement for my writing and have been invaluable in their review of my work.

I should also like to thank members of my immediate family: my brother, Marty Aronoff, for infecting me with his passion for sports; my mother, Bernice Aronoff Zanoff, for her lifelong dedication to the written word; my children, James Richard Karmel and Allison Karmel Thomason, who were so understanding of the explanation "sorry, I've got a game" when it came to their own needs; and to my partner and dearest friend, Robert Pauly, for his continued outstanding critiques of my work and his tolerance and understanding of its importance in my life.

Finally, I would be remiss if I failed to express my gratitude and appreciation for those who made all of this possible. Throughout the long, icy New England winters, the women who have played for the University of Connecticut basketball team have added passion and fire to my life, and for this I am ever grateful.

You've Come a Long Way

In 1902 editors of the student newspaper of the then Connecticut Agricultural College noted that the thirteen "young ladies" of Grove Cottage (the women's dormitory) so enjoyed the men's "athletic contest" of basket ball (sic), they were "led . . . to want a team of their own." This is the first recorded mention of a women's basketball team at the University of Connecticut. It came about a year after the men's team was formed and was made up of—who else?—the "young ladies" of Grove Cottage.

Helen Stimson, the wife of college president Rufus Stimson, was the "manager" and led her team to a season record of 2–0, both victories coming at the expense of the girls of Willimantic High School, 12 miles down the road.

The student newspaper, the *Lookout*, reported the team to be a "lively aggregation of agile young ladies" who took their more experienced opponents by surprise.

"The college girls started in with a vigor amazing to behold," wrote athletic notes editor J. B. Twing. The first recorded basket in history was made on a "pretty throw" by Grace Koons, daughter of the college's president emeritus Benjamin Koons. The final score of that first game was 15–6. The second game showed marked improvement as they beat the same team 25–6, this time on their court. At the time, all field goals were worth 3 points each.

Thus began a campus sport that has been through the ups and downs of victory and defeat, empty stands and sellouts, early exits from seasons, and five national championships.

After it started, the program continued to thrive with a mixture of opponents from city and town recreation clubs to other colleges. In 1920, for example, the team was on a roll. January 7 they defeated the Ludlow Recreation Club of Ludlow, Massachusetts, 8–2. Although the Co-Eds (the team name at the time) won, they didn't play that well, "fumbling the ball repeatedly and missing many opportunities for baskets." One must wonder if the current team didn't take a page out of history, based on this observation from the 1920 campus paper: "They gave Ludlow, however, very few opportunities to score." Even then,

The 1902 women's basketball team.
University of Connecticut Archives

defense had become important in women's basketball at the University of Connecticut.

Four days later the Co-Eds showed they also had an offense, scoring "some fifty odd" points against the Columbian girls of New Haven. "Splendid team work and the ability to cover the floor and arrive at the critical moment at the same time the ball did characterized Connecticut's playing," the campus newspaper reported. Again, a page from the past pointed to the future.

That season, 1920, was the most successful to date, thanks to coach Roy Guyer, who also organized and managed the team. They won five of their first six games, losing only the first game to their old nemesis, Willimantic High School.

The next year, 1921, started a tradition that carried on for decades when the women played the preliminary game for a men's contest. Then called the "Stenogs" (for stenographers, or secretaries), the sparse records indicate they won a fair share of games. They also lost a few because the senior members were off campus at a teacher training course, prohibiting Connecticut from throwing "its strongest combination into the fray." That was also the year that coach-turned-athletic-director Roy Guyer scheduled women's teams from other colleges for the first time. Games were played in the gym on the upper floor at Grove Cottage. In 1924 the transition to an all-college schedule was complete. However, nearly twenty-five years before Title IX, women's basketball underwent a setback when varsity games were replaced by a Guyer idea, called "play days," in which teams from all over the region—high school, recreation club, and so on—came on the same day for a kind of round-robin jamboree. The competition might have been good, but the games did nothing to advance the cause of varsity women's basketball on campus. A few years later, it is recorded in the student newspaper, the women were trounced 25–7 by the Bridgeport High School girls, "as part of the entertainment for the high school men" who were invited to a banquet in Storrs.

Strangely the campus paper is silent about any women's basketball activities until several decades later. In 1955 the Women's Athletic Association (a separate entity from the men's) put in a plea for more athletic activities for women and greater support for those activities. Hawley Armory, where women's sports had been played since they started at the turn of the twentieth century, was woefully inadequate. But despite poor facilities and lack of support, some nine women's sports were played under the WAA's watchful eye.

Sometime in the mid-1950s, the campus newspaper, now called the *Connecticut Campus*, reported that the women's basketball intramurals was opening its season with games between sororities. Missing was mention of the fact that there was a varsity women's basketball team. Pat Robinson, who now lives in Brunswick, Maine, coached that team as well as the field hockey and softball teams (and taught physical education in the department that oversaw the teams) from 1953 to the mid-1960s. For Robinson, a plain-spoken, good-humored woman, there was no off-season.

"We played four games a year, two home and two away," she said. "Two were against regular college teams (Southern Connecticut, Springfield College), and two were those dreaded play days where everybody showed up from every sport."

Robinson said the most skilled players were basketball and softball athletes because those sports were emphasized in the high schools. Field hockey was relatively new. "I loved it," she said. The notion of too much work, of having to dump the field hockey pads and sticks one day for a basketball the next, never bothered her.

And how did they play? "We did all right," Robinson said. "We weren't the caliber they are today, but we had fun . . . we had a really good time. Winning was important but not the major goal. The major goal was to have fun and to play a game, not knock off the other team. But we did all right. We were competitive."

The Entertainers

As part of the entertainment for the high school men
who were invited to the banquet, the co-eds played the
Bridgeport High sextet in Hawley Armory last Saturday
afternoon. Our team appeared to be off form and we
were beaten by a score of 25 to 7. Although our team
played a hard and consistent game they were unable
to break up the teamwork of their opponents. The
co-ed team seemed to have hard luck on all its shots,
as time and again they would roll around the hoop
only to roll off.

—*The* Connecticut Campus, *March 21, 1921*

Funds came from the School of Physical Education and
fund-raisers run by the WAA, like selling balloons at the football
games. Ah, piggybacking the men again.

Robinson said that in those days women weren't beating down
the gym door to play sports. In fact, she assessed recruiting this way:
"We took anybody who came through the door," and there were
enough to field a basketball team of twelve or so. The class of 1965,
one of her last as her coaching career was winding down, was particularly talented, she said, because at least two of them played all
three sports. Like their coach, they had no rest from fall to spring.

Practices were held two afternoons a week from 3:00 to 5:30,
and the usual suspects came to the games: the rest of the phys ed
department, "the matrons from the locker rooms," some parents,
and a few friends.

As the 1960s wore on, women's basketball began to take shape again. Emily Mercer, who also coached in that turbulent decade, recalls having trouble getting enough players to fill the ranks, but those she got were competitive and took the game seriously. Like Robinson, Mercer, who still lives in Storrs, coached more than one sport. "We all kind of shared coaching," she said. When she was coaching, it was not unheard of to play more than one game a day—a regular game and one of Mr. Guyer's play days.

In the first recorded season (1974–75), under head coach Sandra Hamm, the Huskies won only their first two games: the opener against Eastern Connecticut, 12 miles down the road in Willimantic (now a Division III power) and a 39–36 win over Keene State in New Hampshire. Connecticut went 2–8 that year. The next season Wanda Flora took over and the results during her five years averaged seven wins and double-digit losses each season. The student newspaper, the *Connecticut Daily Campus*, pretty much ignored the early Flora years except for a snide comment in December 1975 when a Christmas wish list for coaches appeared. Flora's was said to be: "A new athletic facility solely for the use of women's sports teams. (Then they don't have to take away precious time from the men's sports.)" The next season the paper ran a report of a meeting in which female coaches and athletes aired their grievances with the athletic department (Title IX was now three years old). Complaints ranged from interruptions during games and practices by other athletes to inadequate locker rooms to cheesy or no uniforms. A column by the associate sports editor, with the headline "Women, Women, Women," promised more coverage of women's athletics and apologized for the heretofore cavalier attitude. A small ad for a "male chauvinist pig T-shirt" ran beneath the column.

Ellen Mahoney, who played basketball from 1969 to 1972, remembers the days when she wore a kind of skirtlike outfit instead of shorts. Mahoney, now a physical education teacher at Ledyard High School (where she set state records for winning softball teams) and an assistant softball coach at UConn, said there were all kinds of old wives' tales floating around about females and athletics, one of which suggested too much conditioning could affect a woman's chances for successful childbirth and other silly stuff. At the time, muscles were also taboo for women.

If muscles were frowned on in the early days, scars were worse. Karen Mullins, who played from 1975 to 1978 (the first two years at the Avery Point branch campus), had to plead with athletic department officials to operate on her left knee to correct possible career-ending cartilage problems. The team physician was adamantly against it, warning her that she would be scarred for life, but Mullins insisted. When the right knee developed similar problems, she went through the same rigmarole but won that battle as well. "I told them, 'no, you're wrong. I want to play.'"

Mullins was used to fighting (and winning) battles. She hadn't intended to go to UConn after her first two years at the branch campus. Programs at schools like Springfield College and Southern were more developed, but the Avery Point athletic director made a convincing case that UConn was going to become a national program and "I bought into it," she said. That was in 1977—a full two years before scholarships were available for women, but Mullins didn't accept that. Instead she walked into the UConn athletic director's office and demanded support. For whatever reason, she was given some money from the football program.

"Even though it was not what it is today, the first time you put on a uniform and played for a real coach who motivated you, it was great," she said. She also learned that virtue was its own reward. "If a girl played sports back then, you were a freak. It was never anything you could be proud of."

Unlike Mahoney's years when the team played in the dungeonlike Hawley Armory, Mullins's squads graduated to Guyer Gymnasium (named for coach and athletic director Roy Guyer), which is connected to the Hugh S. Greer Field House (named for a legendary former men's basketball coach), and at least twice they played at the Hartford Civic Center as the opener to a doubleheader with the men. They eventually moved to the field house, a multiuse facility that recently underwent a pricey face-lift. A six-lane track encircled the basketball court, and even when women's games were going on, students and faculty jogged and lifted weights in the corner, the clanking sometimes louder than the fifty or so fans trying to cheer on the team.

None of that mattered. "We were just psyched to play," recalled Mullins. "We weren't playing for fans."

Perhaps the first "star" to play for the UConn women was Cathy Bochaine, a speedy record-setting guard from nearby Plainfield. She chose UConn over Yale University, Boston University, and Boston College, schools whose programs were certainly as well-established, if not more so, than that in Storrs. But being close to her family and pleased with her acceptance into UConn's rigorous pharmacy school (today she is a pharmacist at a CVS in Mansfield—fewer than 2 miles from the campus), she selected Storrs. UConn had just begun offering full rides to female athletes, and the prospect of a free college education was too good to turn down.

An early star: Cathy Bochaine.
University of Connecticut Archives

From 1979 to 1983 Bochaine was a starting guard—good enough as a freshman to bring the ball up. It didn't matter that the stands weren't packed full of cheering fans, that television networks weren't at courtside, that media hordes didn't follow her every move. What mattered was to be able to play at the college level and to be taken seriously as an athlete.

She got a rude awakening in one of her first games, a 5:00 P.M. contest against Yale University, whose men's team was facing the UConn men two hours later as the second half of a double-header. The field house stands were nearly empty (at least they weren't playing at the dreaded Hawley Armory) at the start of the women's game, with only family and a few friends of the players in attendance. As usual, Bochaine's sisters were there with their books, reading through most of the action until Cathy was involved, at which point they'd close their books, cheer, and then pick them up again and resume reading.

This night against Yale, as 7:00 P.M. approached, fans started filtering in for the men's game. They sauntered across the court, apparently unaware that there was another game already in progress. "I'm saying, 'Hey, get off the floor,'" Bochaine recalled. "There's a game going on here." To herself she thought, "Maybe this isn't important to you, but it is to us." Nothing worked as the men's fans continued their march across her basketball court to their seats. With little or no respect from those outside of the circle of players and their small following, athletes like Bochaine, who had earned more respect as a three-year all-state player at tiny Plainfield High School in northeastern Connecticut, discovered once again that in women's basketball, virtue was its own reward. Bochaine, in particular, was a gym rat. Every spare moment was spent in Guyer shooting baskets—an environment that smelled of sweat and resounded of sneaker screeches, an environment that for her was like home.

But the struggle continued. From the 1974–75 season through 1985–86, Connecticut had only one winning season in eleven. Even coach Geno Auriemma couldn't reverse that trend in his inaugural season. But finally, in his second year (1986–87), he led the Huskies to a 14–13 record, and they have not had a losing season since.

Prior to Auriemma, the one winning season was 1980–81, when they went 16–14 under head coach Jean Balthaser. She was replaced by Auriemma as the university made a commitment to beef up its women's basketball program. (Both field hockey and soccer were already national powers, advancing regularly to the elite levels of the NCAA tournaments.) During that one pre-Auriemma winning season, the Huskies had a decisive overtime victory over then power Boston University; their schedule included nationally ranked teams such as Southern Connecticut State University and Springfield College, schools that dominated the women's basketball scene years before the rise of Tennessee, Louisiana Tech, Old Dominion, and Auburn.

Bochaine, a sophomore, was on that winning team. "That year I remember thinking, 'Hey, school's a breeze,' then I got a D on my first calculus test," she said. That would become problematic later in her college career when she saw her basketball days waning, but for now, her team was winning. Life was good.

It was to be short-lived. Her junior year the team was wracked with injuries, and a handful of players—whose winning year opened doors for them—transferred to schools with better basketball programs. The team was so decimated that although she was only 5'8" and on the light side, Bochaine had to play power

The Full-court Press

These days the UConn women's basketball media guide for
the press is a nearly 300-page glossy book with color photo-
graphs, statistics, biographies, recaps of tournaments, and
just about every piece of information the media may need in
covering the team. There are pages and pages of information
and background on the players, especially the stars, starting
with their high-school records and working up to the previous
season. Pictures of players posed in lovely outfits as well as a
host of action shots make the media guide fun to read.

But back in the 1978–79 season, the "media guide"
consisted of two printed pages, folded in half, with just the
bare necessities. A sample: "Wanda Ward: 5'3" sophomore
guard from Bridgton, Me. . . . playmaker who impressed in
spot duty as a freshman . . . third in free throw percentage,
fourth in assists." This was accompanied by a head shot.

forward in some games. "There was no one in practice to push
me," she said. "I really don't think I got any better after my sophomore year." ·

Nevertheless, as a Husky, Bochaine set records for scoring
(1,534 points) and steals (240). When in 1991 Kerry Bascom
broke her scoring record (2,177 points), Bochaine said, "It felt
like little pieces of my experience at UConn were being eroded."
But she knew it was inevitable . . . that the program was growing
and destined for greater heights.

Another player who had a vision of what was to come was Renee Najarian, who transferred from South Carolina her sophomore year to be closer to her family in Wakefield, Massachusetts. Auriemma had recruited Najarian, a highly regarded inside player, when he was an assistant at the University of Virginia, but she didn't think she'd get the playing time she would with the Gamecocks, so she headed for the Southeastern Conference school instead. When she finally got to play at UConn (1986–88) after more than a year of sitting on the bench to conform to NCAA regulations for transfers, she quickly made a mark, averaging 17.1 points and 10.1 rebounds a game. "I didn't transfer to Connecticut to be part of a national power," she said. "We just wanted a winning season." Her freshman year, Auriemma brought in two outstanding recruits: Bascom, from the small town of Epping, New Hampshire, and Laura Lishness from Bristol, one of the best Connecticut athletes to ever play the game. "We were still disjointed and were losing close games by 3 or 4 points, so we were not over the hump yet," recalled Najarian, who is now an assistant athletic director at E. O. Smith High School, adjacent to the UConn campus in Mansfield. "And I wasn't the greatest leader at that time. I had some growing up to do."

Najarian said the players and coaching staff always entered a game expecting to win, even though that was not always realistic. "But the coaches had the right vision, the right plan," she said of Auriemma and his assistant Chris Dailey, still a team today.

Najarian knew that Connecticut had reached another level, however, when two years after her playing days were over, she witnessed a Connecticut victory over Final Four power Auburn in the field house. "I remember thinking 'Wow they just beat Auburn.'" That same year the Huskies made their first trip to the

Final Four. Since then they've been there seven more times, bringing back five national championship trophies. Peggy Walsh, one of the better players to ever block a shot at Connecticut (she played from 1982 to 1986), remembers watching the 1991 Final Four team and thinking, "Wow, Geno got them there quick."

When they decided to turn the keys of the kingdom over to this bright young coach, did even the UConn athletic department honchos have any idea what was in store? No doubt, Geno Auriemma exceeded even their desires, which at the time, would have been as simple as a winning season.

Geno-ius of Gampel

Geno Auriemma arrived in Storrs in a battered two-toned blue Mercury Bobcat that was missing a muffler. Who knows? Perhaps the noise it made as it pulled onto the University of Connecticut campus was an indication of the cheering that was to come his way not too far down the road.

His introduction to Storrs was in May 1985, and the Bobcat belonged to Cathy Bochaine, a former player and member of the search committee that was reviewing candidates to replace Jean Balthaser, who had only one winning season in the five years she coached from 1980 to 1985.

"I'll be wearing a blue jacket, white shirt, and red tie," Auriemma told Bochaine over the phone as they made arrangements for her to pick him up at the airport.

Unlike other members of the search committee, Bochaine didn't have strong feelings one way or another about whether Balthaser's replacement should be a female. There were those who felt the job should go to a woman to make the players feel more comfortable and to provide a role model.

Sometime between the salad and the coffee at a local steak house, Bochaine was won over by this young assistant coach at the University of Virginia who had outgrown his role as the number two man to Debbie Ryan. "By the end of the night I thought he could sell my Bobcat," Bochaine recalls.

Auriemma's gift of salesmanship also helped convince then Connecticut athletic director John Toner that he was right for the job. A year later, Toner was to hire another bright young star in the coaching firmament in Boston-bred Jim Calhoun, a highly successful men's basketball coach at Northeastern University and a New Englander through and through.

Auriemma was none of that. In the first place, he wasn't even born in this country, and in the second place, when his family came over from Italy (he was eight), they settled in the Philadelphia suburb of Norristown, where flocks of Italian-American immigrants gathered, keeping one foot in the old country and one in the new. Auriemma was the foot in the new world, representing his parents in the marketplace, in banks, to real estate salesmen because among the five of them (he has a sister and a brother), he was the only one who spoke English well enough to communicate with the outside world.

His parents' decision to leave the comfort zone of Montella,

Geno Auriemma shouts instructions from the bench.
Willimantic Chronicle/*Ken Sayers*

their tiny rural village east of Naples, his early experiences as the outsider, and his struggle to assimilate and become successful in one of the areas in which he excelled have shaped the man, now fifty-one, into a hard-nosed survivor with unwavering standards and a visceral repulsion to those who don't try.

"The two of them came across the ocean to make a name for themselves and establish their family, to give their kids a chance — to do more than they had done," he says of his mother Marsiela and his father, Donato, who died nearly a decade ago, at sixty-nine, of cancer. Certainly, in Auriemma's case, his success has more than exceeded their ambitions for him — last year he signed a five-year $4.8 million contract. He has become successful through a heavy dose of native intelligence, a keen sense of humor, hard work, self-confidence, and a driving ambition to be the best in his field. Five national championships since 1995 only tell half the story.

Auriemma is also an accomplished media analyst and motivational speaker and has the enviable ability of knowing how to take care of number one. That became clear when he interviewed with Toner that sunny day in May 1985. Although Auriemma needed his stamp of approval (the search committee made the final decision), he impressed Toner enough so that the powerful president of the NCAA was in his corner from the start.

"I felt that he would recruit well and impress the parents," Toner said, referring to Auriemma's gift of expressing himself in a down-to-earth humorous way. "His strong love of family and belief in women's basketball convinced me there would be no problem" with gender.

Toner was also impressed with the way Auriemma said he'd treat his players. He doesn't distinguish between female and male basketball players; basketball should be played in a certain way by both genders, and that's the way he expects it to be done on his team. If women are more reticent to grab leadership roles, are more pensive rather than instinctive on the court, display more emotional extremes, they have to try to overcome these qualities if they're going to succeed in his world. Of Diana Taurasi, the best he's ever had, he used to say, "She plays like a guy."

The issue of a male coach could have been a touchy one with feminists, Title IX advocates, and others questioning why a woman wasn't hired for the job. The number of successful women coaching other women in the sport was small (Debbie Ryan, Jody Conradt at Texas, Pat Summitt at Tennessee, Theresa Grentz then at Rutgers, recently retired Sue Gunter at LSU), and the chance to create a role model for future coaches was tempting.

Pat Meiser-McKnett, then UConn associate athletic director for women's sports who chaired the search committee and was a former basketball coach at Penn State, said the gender issue started out being important to her. "Obviously I was going to support a woman candidate anytime I could, but then we sat with the team and got feedback about what they wanted in a coach, and it was clear to me they didn't care," she said. "When I heard that, I decided they were the group we needed to please, so if it was not important to them, then it was not important to me."

Meiser-McKnett, now the athletic director at the University of Hartford, said Auriemma was the last candidate interviewed in a string of highly qualified coaches, most of them female. But Auriemma had set things in motion before his campus visit by making contact with significant people in the life of each member on the search committee. "When Bob Cousy calls Dee Rowe (an associate athletic director) and says you have to talk to

And Don't Forget the Alka-Seltzer

Geno Auriemma was raised on the best Italian cooking known to the world: his mom's. So when pressed to name what he would order on the proverbial desert island, naturally he said his mother's eggplant parmigiana, her lasagna, and a bottle of Barolo wine, a full-bodied red from the Piemonte region of Italy (Auriemma is a wine expert and collects the stuff). A good cup of espresso would top off the meal.

"When you start cooking at ten with only homemade ingredients, picked out back and made on your counter, it's pretty hard to get that wrong," he said of his mother's tomato sauce. "After you do it for sixty years, you don't get it wrong either."

Auriemma's mother, seventy-one-year-old Marsiela, still lives in Norristown, Pennsylvania, where the family settled when they came to this country nearly fifty years ago. But she visits her son in Manchester, Connecticut, frequently, staying for a month or two at a time. Her diminutive figure and kind face are a frequent presence in the coach's row of seats behind the bench at the Hartford Civic Center and across the court when they play at Gampel.

By the way, the rest of the world may someday enjoy his mother's recipes as much as her family has for so many years. Auriemma has plans to open an Italian restaurant in downtown Hartford as soon as a suitable location can be found. In June 2005 he announced plans to open Geno Auriemma's Fast Break, an international food court at the Mohegan Sun Casino in Uncasville, Connecticut.

this guy . . . ," Meiser-McKnett's voice trails off, but the implication is clear: You have to talk to this guy.

"For me, it was Debbie Ryan," she said referring to a call from Auriemma's boss at the time. Ryan told her Auriemma was the reason the Cavaliers went from the "bottom to the top," referring to his considerable recruiting skills.

"So when he finally got to the table," Meiser-McKnett continued, "he already had a foot in the door. It was very clear he had a great style, that he could identify and recruit talent because he had done it down there." She said the committee (only one person opposed his hiring) was won over by his inner confidence and easy style. "He wasn't the 6'5" guy with his arms crossed across his chest staring down at you. His arms are always open, always out, he smiles, he makes people feel comfortable." The search committee recommended him to the athletic director, who needed no convincing that Geno Auriemma was the man for the job.

And so in the fall of 1985, he began a journey that would lead to unprecedented success—success that at times has even caught him a little off guard.

According to Toner, an interesting footnote is that if Auriemma had turned down UConn, the offer would have gone to Chris Dailey, then an assistant coach at her alma mater, Rutgers, which she helped lead to a national championship as a player in 1982. As it worked out, they had it both ways when Dailey signed on as Geno's assistant. They have been together ever since. In many ways Chris Dailey keeps the trains running. Besides handling hotels and restaurants, she instructs players on post defense and is constantly on their case about off-the-court matters such as dressing appropriately for public appearances and keeping their uniform shirts tucked in at all times. Daily is also responsible for the recruiting correspondence, especially with parents. She is polite almost to a fault, the perfect polish for the diamond in the rough that is Auriemma. And he couldn't run the show without her.

What the two of them inherited two decades ago was a team of average talent not ever pushed hard enough, a team of women from comfortable middle-class homes, most of whom were smart and tired of losing. Most were from Connecticut or neighboring states; most went on to become successful professionals and are now settled down with families, heading into middle age. Auriemma hears from them regularly and includes them in alumni and other events revolving around the team. With few exceptions, he is loyal to them, and they are loyal to him.

His first and most formidable task was to teach these young women that they could win. Through his first season he went 12–15 (it remains his only losing season at Connecticut). With the exception of the 1980–81 season when Balthaser went 16–14, a dozen victories were more than had ever been recorded in UConn women's history, dating back to 1974–75 when records were first kept. The stories of how the team played in the leaky, drafty field house, with rarely more than a hundred family members and friends present, are legendary. Auriemma's office was a box off of a depressingly dark corridor to the rear of the court. Postgame conferences were held in the hall, with Auriemma leaning up against the wall and one or two sportswriters asking him about how hard the kids tried. Today's news conferences are conducted in a special room at Gampel Pavilion with banks of television cameras and at least fifteen beat reporters a game. Still, Auriemma respected the players' efforts: At that time, the notion of a highly gifted player who could turn a program around was still a pipe dream.

Peggy Walsh, the best player that Auriemma inherited, said they didn't handle the ball once during the first two weeks of practice under the new regime. All they did were defensive drills. "My legs hurt so much I had to take the elevator to my dorm room," she said. It was on the first floor. Walsh, who was lured to Connecticut from New Jersey by Cathy Bochaine, said at first she was nervous about the new coach. But she saw immediately he could make her a better player and that the team could win. Which they did, opening the 1985–86 season 7–0 (including a win over Syracuse, a powerful Big East team at the time); the players and the coach were overjoyed. Walsh, who works part-time in the women's basketball office handling fan mail and other aspects of the program, is third in all-time rebounding (937) and fourth in average (8.7 per game) and in career blocks (162).

"We worked harder than we had ever worked before. Everyone respected him; we didn't want to let him down," she said. The magnetism he held over the team, the charisma, has worked for years for Geno Auriemma. Although it may be tested more these days because of the difference between this generation and what he was used to, his charm, his directness, his standards still bring out the best in players willing to put in the effort.

It soon became clear that if he was going to build something, he'd have to go outside the borders of the state to find good players. The UConn Athletic Division, then committed to spending lots of money to build the program (it was clear women's basketball was turning into the elite sport for the gender), gave him a healthy recruiting budget and he started combing the East Coast.

In 1987 he found that first highly gifted player in a tiny New Hampshire town in the person of Kerry Bascom, who hardly looked the part of an elite athlete but, as far as the coach was

Geno Auriemma cut down the nets after the 2003 national championship.
University of Connecticut Division of Athletics

concerned, had a blue-collar work ethic and desire to succeed—qualities he had grown up with among the concrete workers and bricklayers of his parents' generation. Bascom was also the first real example of one of Auriemma's greatest talents: that of spotting a future star who may be under the radar of other coaches. To complement Bascom, he did find an elite athlete in Laura Lishness, one of the best state players to ever attend UConn. Though frighteningly talented, the quirky star (who is prominent on UConn top ten career and single-season record lists—oddly enough for assists and blocks) was moody and stubborn. The two frequently locked horns—a scenario that would play itself out over and over again with others in the years to come. After securing Bascom and Lishness, he went back to his roots, to small communities of Pennsylvania where he had developed contacts through his years as a high-school and college coach in that area. The work of finding the quality nonstate players had begun. Once the gates were opened, the best of their senior classes flocked to Storrs. High-school players of the year, glittering with trophies and individual state records, came to play; but so did lesser-known players whose work ethic and devotion to team play landed them a spot on the team and national championship rings.

Success breeds success and, in college sports, money. The money has flowed in to the program—much of it from television revenues and ticket sales. For road games, players and coaches fly charter so they're not wasting time sitting around airports; they stay at luxury hotels, eat at five-star restaurants, and have other amenities to add to the mystique of playing at UConn. When she graduated in 2005, Ashley Valley, who didn't play that much in her four years, said she lived better than she ever will when she's

The Pick of the Picks

In 2005 as the women's program noted the tenth anniversary of the Connecticut-Tennessee regular season series, Geno Auriemma was asked to recount his top five moments in games with the Lady Vols. Some determined the outcome of a particular game; others had larger implications for the season—and, of course, the rivalry. Here they are, in no particular order:

1. Jen Rizzotti takes the ball coast to coast in the final seconds of the 1995 national championship game to give UConn its first national title. "That was the ultimate moment," Auriemma said.
2. Nykesha Sales hits a three-pointer with 4 seconds left to send the 1996 national semifinal in Charlotte, North Carolina, into overtime. The Lady Vols prevailed 88–83. "That was as much fun as I've had as a coach," Auriemma said.
3. Semeka Randall makes a buzzer shot (she had 2 three-pointers in the final minutes) to beat the Huskies at Gampel February 2. Randall, a tough, physical player, picked up the nickname "Boo" after that because of the reaction of UConn fans.
4. The following season, Randall again prompted a greatest moment when she injured Svetlana Abrosimova during a tussle over a rebound in Knoxville in 2001, ending Abrosimova's college career. "Do they still hate me?" Randall asked recently of UConn fans, who booed her when Michigan State beat the Huskies last season. She is an assistant coach with the Spartans.
5. This one's a toss-up between Diana Taurasi's three-point shot at the buzzer to give Connecticut a 1-point win over the Lady Vols in Hartford. Taurasi also hit a shot from midcourt.
                                    OR
    Rizzotti's pass to Jamelle Elliott in the lane that resulted in a three-point play during a January 1996 game in Knoxville that ended Tennessee's record-setting sixty-nine-game home winning streak. "At that moment, I knew we had won the game," Auriemma said of the pass from Elliott, who is now one of his assistant coaches.

out in the working world: "Heck, I got free trips to Hawaii, San Antonio, New Orleans; I got to stay in the best hotels, eat the best meals." And she has three national championship rings to boot.

But all of this luxury comes at a price. Although maturation and experience have softened him ever so slightly over the years, Auriemma is still a man of strong will who takes it as a challenge to bend players to his way of thinking. In his younger days, even with far less skilled athletes, he was relentless in this pursuit: If Bascom couldn't shoot free throws, he made sure during the summer that's all she did. If Debbie Baer was a poor shooter, he turned her into a first-rate defensive player who may only take one shot a game, but rarely let the player she guarded have any good ones.

Through the years, with few exceptions, players have praised his fairness. And even though he's on the other side of fifty, he can still get most of his players to respond, whether to his charm or his basketball knowledge, or both. But while some coaches may promise recruits the moon, Auriemma is painfully straight with them, making it clear that all the talent on earth won't guarantee them a spot in the rotation if they don't work hard. Over the years, he has benched some of the best players he's ever coached (Diana Taurasi, Svetlana Abrosimova, Shea Ralph) because they didn't work hard in practice leading up to a game or didn't listen to him when he was trying to make them even better. He says often that the wins and the losses aren't as important to him as the way the game is played. "I'm a fan of good basketball more than I'm a fan of winning basketball," he'll frequently say after his team has blown out an opponent more because of the latter's poor play than UConn's good play.

Sometimes his quest for perfection may take him too far. One afternoon during her senior year, he was so hard on Sue

Bird during practice, she left the court crying and, though normally the most cooperative athlete, refused to participate in the standard postpractice Q&A with the media. Bird was a strong player; she never pouted even when she had to sit out her freshman year with a torn knee ligament. But this day, Auriemma had crossed a line. Afterward he acknowledged he had been too hard on her—perhaps he didn't get a good night's sleep, or he had a fight with one of his own kids (he has two daughters, both at UConn, and a son in high school). Or more likely, because she was so good and worked so hard, he expected just a little too much of her that day. That's the way with the best—standards are a little higher for them, there are no free passes, and if he thinks they come up short—if just for a brief time in practice—they pay for their mistakes.

No doubt, at the next practice, Bird played harder than she ever had. When he benched Shea Ralph in the first half of a game against Rhode Island, the popular player bore the temporary banishment bravely, as she sat on the bench an eyeblink away from tears. When he figured the lesson had sunk in and put her back in the game, she scored 15 points in twelve minutes in the second half. That's the way with many of his players: So driven to accomplishment and so eager to show him he was wrong, they sometimes achieve beyond their own expectations.

Even in his first year, the rules were clear. Walsh, head and shoulders the best player on the 1985–86 team, remembers him calling her into his office and telling her if there was a game the next day, she would have been benched because he didn't like her practice habits. "From that day on I knew to take practice seriously," she said. "He hasn't changed since that first year. He's the same guy he was when he was making $29,000."

In most cases Auriemma is a master at pushing the right buttons: He goes toe to toe with stubborn talented players; he ignores them if they ignore his instruction; he makes public comments about their deficiencies; and occasionally, if all else fails, he has heart-to-heart meetings with players to set the record straight. (Unless the issue is compelling, such as the illness of a parent, he refuses to get involved in his players' personal lives. That is for others to deal with—assistant coaches, other players. His concern is how they play.) A few can't take the demands and expectations and they leave, but usually they lacked the talent to play at the elite level to begin with or were so hung up on the way he treated them, they were emotionally unable to continue. Water finds its natural level; the transfers usually find a school and coach more to their temperament and everything ends happily.

"Coach always has your best interests in mind," said Taurasi. "You think he's against you but he has your best interests. I didn't understand that for three years, but I learned it."

A few principles have guided Auriemma through his life and his career. For example, he is fond of saying a person's "greatest strength is their greatest weakness." If Diana Taurasi decided, for example, that she preferred to pass rather than shoot on a given day, there was not much he could do about it, even if her points were needed at the time. Her desire to make those around her better was certainly a strength, but at times it was also a drawback.

One of his own greatest strengths and therefore greatest weaknesses is his delight in holding forth with the media, a banter that combines the one-liners of a stand-up comic, blunt assessments of his and other players, and, occasionally, political or sociological references that land with a thud, like a basketball with the air taken out of it. Last year he criticized the fans,

Geno Auriemma with his 2002 graduates, from left: Swin Cash, Asjha Jones, Sue Bird, and Jamika Williams. University of Connecticut Division of Athletics

shocked by a UConn loss, for acting as if they were at a golf match. Several years ago, he publicly criticized a UConn student newspaper reporter for asking a tough question after a loss and then had to publicly apologize; he has made fun of Tennessee coach Pat Summitt, a more aloof individual who respects his coaching ability but once said they don't talk on the phone; and on more than one occasion, he publicly declared that this or that player will never wear a UConn uniform again—only to have to praise her a week later when she had an outstanding game (it worked, is what he might say). "As a public figure I have to come to grips with the fact that everything I do and say does take on a whole other level," he said. "If I make a comment on a social issue, it's different than if a guy working at Pratt & Whitney makes that comment." But it never stops him.

Although his team keeps delivering when it counts, the past few years he has struggled with larger matters involving the personnel coming out of high school and being delivered to his doorstep. He's frustrated with players who have what he calls a sense of entitlement, who think once they put on the Connecticut jersey, a national championship or All-America trophy will magically appear. (His well-furnished suite of offices just a few hundred yards from the basketball court already has more hardware than Lowe's.) Sometimes he takes responsibility for his intolerance, but then quickly dismisses that. "I'm being asked to accept much more than before," he said. "It's a tug of war—who gives first? And I don't want to give in."

The lack of effort on the part of increasing numbers of players, and the failure of high school and AAU coaches to stress the basics will be the things that finally drive him out of the profession. "If anything would, it would be that feeling that you have to cater to your players in terms of their individual wishes and their whims instead of them giving of themselves to the group. I've never glorified the individual (UConn players' names aren't on the back of their jerseys), but today a kid comes in with a sense of entitlement."

He was tested most recently by Charde Houston, a very talented player from California (she broke Cheryl Miller's state high-school scoring record her senior year at San Diego High School). Houston is a great offensive player—and this seemed to be all she was willing to do—go to the basket—for much of her rookie season. Auriemma tried everything: benching her, insulting her publicly ("She has the ball maybe four minutes a game; what does she do the other thirty-six?" he once wondered aloud), talking with her, having the upperclassmen talk to her— nothing seemed to work. She tired easily both in practice and in games. Finally, he was convinced (he needed the points, frankly) to let her play through her mistakes, and though she had an up-and-down first season—most freshmen do—she was a far better player in March, understanding what it really means to wear the UConn jersey, than she was in October. The young coach might have kept her on the bench until she did a 360 in practice; the older, wiser coach let it run its course.

Like the best and brightest of his players, Auriemma is a stand-up guy who takes responsibility for his actions. But he is also a man molded by his background and experiences of being at one time a stranger in a strange land; of being a hard worker but too short (5'10") and not athletic enough to play at the highest levels; of being an outspoken, supremely confident individual who refuses to compromise on basics.

"I never got things I wanted without working for them, yet at the same time I expected to achieve to a certain level," he says.

There are plenty of people who resent Geno Auriemma: He can be arrogant, insulting, disdainful, and blunt to a fault. "Sometimes I wish he had a little more positive reinforcement for players," Walsh said. But he has never represented himself as anything other than what he is. "We are what we are," he says frequently about his team. And he is what he is.

In many ways, despite his wealth, his facility with language, his sense of humor, his sense of style, his devotion to good wine and good food, his ease on golf courses at private country clubs, Geno Auriemma is still the bold young kid just off the boat

An Impossible Task

If you ask Geno Auriemma to pick his best team of all time, he shakes his head and lets you know it can't be done. Sure the 2002 team (Cash, Bird, Taurasi, Jones, Williams) at 39-0 may have been woman for woman the best five he's ever assembled, but then how do you leave off Rebecca Lobo? Jamelle Elliott? Jen Rizzotti? Kara Wolters? Nykesha Sales? Svetlana Abrosimova? Shea Ralph? These are the imponderables that finally leave him with this conclusion: "That's impossible." And then: "I've been fortunate to coach so many great players . . . most coaches can easily answer that question, but I can't."

hoping to catch a piece of the American dream. "It's every man for himself," he said one day when reflecting on how his past has shaped him. "People weren't knocking on my door and handing me things. There were no ESL classes in my school, no signs in Italian in my neighborhood. We couldn't afford a car so we didn't have one until I was in tenth grade. But back then you just did what you needed to do and moved on. I tell my kids 'I worked hard for everything I got. You need to, too. Life doesn't owe you a thing. You owe life your best effort.'"

Despite all he has accomplished, his is a restless spirit, never satisfied with his level of achievement. The dream is still out there—fading a little with age, experience, and changes he can't control, but that desire to add yet one more national championship trophy to the office shelf shines as brightly as the gold of the trophy itself.

The CPTV Phenomenon

"Backing in: 10-9-8-7-6-5-4-3-2-1," the time-out coordinator shouts to the half-dozen production personnel assembled in the truck. "Have a good show," Lori Mancini calls out, much like a coach tells his or her team to have a good game before the huddle breaks for the court. The UConn and University of South Florida women's lineups flash on the screens—tip-off is a second away.

Lori Mancini's command post is a large white truck, with the words GAME CREEK printed across the side, that sits outside and to the rear of Gampel Pavilion. Inside the truck the technical and production staff of Connecticut Public Television, the public broadcasting station for the state, works at a frenzied pace to televise each UConn women's basketball game. Over the years it has become the lifeline to the sold-out Huskies for thousands of fans across the region. Typically, it takes some twenty-four people to staff a home game, including announcers, statisticians, technical support, and coordinators. CPTV also goes on the road with the team (with a much smaller staff) and has not missed a game in close to a decade unless ESPN or CBS has prior rights.

The fact that all of the regular-season games are televised has been a huge draw to the top-flight recruits that come to visit and often decide to play in Storrs. How many other women's basketball programs can tell newcomers that their every basket, their every rebound, their every assist will be watched by adoring fans throughout the state and the nation and, thanks to live Internet streaming, throughout the world?

During a game, the pace of the action in the truck — graphics, tape replays, live commentary, promos for the station — is every bit as fast and furious as the stuff going on down the back stairs and through the hallway to the court.

CPTV's pregame routines follow a pattern: Two hours before the start, Mancini, who has produced the games for six years; play-by-play announcer Bob Picozzi; and color analyst Meghan Pattyson-Cuomo meet with the rest of the TV crew for a quick bite and final discussions of the important aspects of that night's encounter. Mancini has already prepared the opening. If the Huskies are struggling, she may emphasize turnovers; if they're on a roll, their defense. Sometimes it's a player—a freshman point guard for example—who is the feature in the lead-in. She tells the announcers what she's put together so that their commentary is in synch with the tape that will run. Mancini has done her homework: This night against the University of South Florida, which will enter the Big East a year hence, the best player is sophomore Jessica Dickson, the leading freshman scorer in the nation last season with an average 18.6 points a game. Several weeks later, they are televising a much-awaited game against number ten–ranked Michigan State University at the Hartford Civic Center; at the time, the Spartans were on the move, and the Huskies, ranked eleventh, were dithering. Mancini knew she had to prepare her viewers for the unthinkable—a UConn loss.

> Mancini orders the crew to wait to show the coaches' stats "on the first dead ball, starting with the USF coach." "Is it South Florida or USF?" a graphic guy shouts at Mancini, who is camped at a long table in front of a bank of TV screens (for live action, taped stuff, station promos, and the like). "South Florida first and then USF," she responds quickly and authoritatively.

The graphics people—called "fonts" in the business—must get that straight and be consistent. What they type into a computer (ANN STROTHER IS 3 FOR 3 FROM LONG RANGE, for example) is what the viewers see seconds later flashed across the bottom of their television screens—screens in tony wood-paneled family rooms in Litchfield County, in quiet, antiseptic nursing homes in West Hartford, in dorm rooms of cheering fans in Storrs, in low-rent projects in Bridgeport. The UConn women's team cuts across age groups, incomes, races.

At the outset it was a risky decision by Connecticut Public Television to mix in a little sport with the likes of dramatic histories of British royalty, endangered pelicans in the Everglades, and hard-hitting *Frontline* exposés of Chilean president Pinochet. It had never been done for any other team in the country and, despite the success, remains unique in sports programming—most likely because of UConn's year-in and year-out winning record and five national championships in a decade. In addition the state has no professional franchises to drain fan resources.

CPTV senior vice president for programming Larry Rifkin estimates for a big game (that ESPN hasn't grabbed up) the station averages a rating of 10.6 (18 percent share of the market), but it has gone as high as 13 percent (23 percent share) if it's a huge game such as during the Big East tournament. "It's the highest rated program in any (PBS) market," says Rifkin. "No one gets the numbers like it does."

> Mancini gives orders to the camera chief, "25 green has 14 points . . . if you want to iso her out of the huddle," telling his crew to go in for a close-up of the phenom Jessica Dickson. It's not exactly the kind of command Auriemma might give Barbara Turner to keep her hands up on defense, but Mancini's directions to her team may be as crucial in some ways to the success of the UConn women's basketball team as anything that comes out of Auriemma's mouth because of the exposure the team gets.

During the 2004–05 season, CPTV started "streaming" games to the Internet so fans who don't get the in-state CPTV broadcasts could tune in, opening up an entirely new market of national and international viewers. The season package cost

$39.95, and early figures showed at least 1,000 customers in forty-five states were buying it. "We're literally worldwide now," said Harriet Unger, the CPTV executive producer in charge of the women's basketball programming.

Though he's modest (he takes as much pride in the fact that he introduced Barney the purple dinosaur to a national PBS organization nearly fifteen years ago), Rifkin is the brains behind CPTV's 1994 decision to broadcast a UConn Big East tournament final against Seton Hall at Gampel Pavilion. "Since it was just one game, we didn't have to risk a lot so we said, 'Let's give it a whirl.' We went on the air that night and although it wasn't total magic, it was enough to maintain our curiosity about what this all held for the future," he says. But it became magic quickly. After Rebecca Lobo hit a driving layup in that Seton Hall game, "the phones lit up with people calling to make a pledge. That ringing hasn't stopped in over a decade," he said.

Two key moves over the next five years sealed the deal with UConn, already anxious to market its winning product. First, in 1995 CPTV management won the bid on the whole package of games UConn was making available instead of working out a shared arrangement with commercial stations. The station caught a big break when the team went 35–0 that year and captured its first national championship. So with a large audience in place, in 1996 the station could commit to televising every game available (about forty hours of air time), which landed them a long-term contract.

This season they are entering the third year of a five-year contract that will run through 2007–08. Under the agreement, CPTV paid the university a fee of $600,000 in the first year; this fee will escalate to $1 million in the final year of the agreement

Meghan Pattyson-Cuomo (left) interviewing Ann Strother. University of Connecticut Division of Athletics

in exchange for the rights to televise at least seventeen games a season, including all home regular-season games and some Big East tournament games. In all, UConn will make some $4 million from the deal, and in return CPTV is counting on viewer pledges to help pay for other programming as well as the cost of televising the games. The contract is exclusive to CPTV, which is what the station has insisted upon since the negotiations began in earnest in 1995.

Since the first year, the broadcasts have been totally dependent on public pledges; CPTV management has not kicked in any of its money. During televised pledge nights and halftime of the games, the promise of UConn women's game coverage is the high point of the sometimes otherwise annoying requests for call-in donations. Tickets to games, merchandise, and other paraphernalia associated with the team are other incentives to viewers to keep their dollars coming in.

"Back live at the Civic Center where UConn has trailed for the first time at the half all season." Bob Picozzi is giving the depressing news to viewers that Michigan State, as expected, is making it tough for Connecticut to get into any offensive rhythm. "Good factoid," chimes in Pattyson-Cuomo. "Show the drought graphic," barks Mancini, and within seconds "0–7 3:41 min" flashes across the bottom of the screen. "Stay with Geno." Director Shawn Jensen, his white U.S. Open baseball cap shoved to the back of his skull, commands a cameraman to get a close-up of the glum coach. Jensen is quicker than the refs—and often the coaches and the athletes—in his ability to spot a significant play developing. "Offensive foul," he shouts as UConn's powerful forward Willnett Crockett barrels into Michigan State's Kelli Roehrig early in the second half, squandering yet another chance for her team to cut into what is now a nine-point lead. Jensen's voice is still echoing in the small truck as the referee blows her whistle and hands the ball to Roehrig waiting on the baseline to complete the turnover. "Get Geno," Jensen barks, and again, the grim face of the coach, his hands tearing through his hair, fills the bank of screens in the truck. "Crockett went in with reckless abandon," Pattyson-Cuomo quips. "I've got all their albums," Jensen remarks to no one in particular, displaying the kind of gallows humor that helps relieve tensions associated with high-anxiety jobs.

In some way the game coverage is just the tip of the iceberg in Connecticut Public Television's women's basketball coverage. It has devoted considerable resources above and beyond the games to the team, which has become its bread and butter programming as far as fund-raising is concerned. The CPTV Web site for UConn women's basketball is as elaborate and complete as any the university puts up—and, in fact, contains multiple one-click links to UConn data such as rosters, bios, stats, box scores, wire reports of the previous games, and other useful information. Perhaps the most popular link, however, is the "Ask Harriet" connection, an e-mail form that viewers may use to send questions to Harriet Unger, who will answer them herself or pass them along to Pattyson-Cuomo to throw at head coach Geno Auriemma during the half-hour *Geno Auriemma Show* that airs before many game telecasts.

The format of the coach's show, taped in CPTV's new headquarters on Asylum Avenue in the heart of Hartford, has Pattyson-Cuomo asking Auriemma about past and upcoming games with little held back. If the team has played poorly, she goes at him. If they're clicking, she's not reticent about praising him and his players. "When they play lousy, it's harder to interview him," she said. "But most of the time it helps that I know him." Pattyson-Cuomo is secure in her role as devil's advocate to Auriemma. As a player she was on the first Final Four team in 1991, and she has remained tight with the program, the players, and the Auriemma family. Never the most talented player on the team and constantly plagued by shoulder problems, she epitomized the toughness and refuse-to-lose attitude that have come to be emblematic of the team and were carried to their extreme in players like Jen Rizzotti and Jamelle Elliott several years later. For two years after she graduated, Pattyson-Cuomo was an assistant coach to Auriemma, but when she realized that was not what she wanted to do, she started casting around for another line of work. She happened to be at the right place at the right time, and CPTV gave her a chance.

"They threw me right in," the popular wise-cracking former player said of her first broadcast. "The first game I ever did I was standing next to (then play-by-play) Mike Gorman, and I know I looked like a complete freak. Mike put the microphone down and told me, 'Just pretend the camera is a third person and you're talking to it.'" It was the best advice she ever received and almost instantly turned her into a smooth, professional announcer who has found the magic combination of education and entertainment for her audience.

Picozzi points out that since Pattyson-Cuomo played for Auriemma—whose demands and expectations have changed very little in his twenty years in Storrs—she knows what's likely to make him angry at his team, even if they come away with the W. "She played and coached there so she has a deep knowledge of the program and the personalities," says Picozzi. "I can't bring that element to the game . . . I'm the sponge."

A longtime local television sportscaster who six years ago switched to ESPN morning radio, Picozzi also does play-by-play for Big East games on ESPN Regional TV—including the few UConn men's games not televised on ESPN or CBS. Although he has done many other sports on the air, Picozzi said his first

The Shoes, the Gum, and the Bun

Throughout the season CPTV women's basketball executive producer Harriet Unger is besieged with e-mails from viewers about the broadcasts. (There is an "Ask Harriet" link on the CPTV women's basketball home page, and e-mails are also sent to the coach to be read during his pregame show.) They range from complaints and praise for the announcers ("I can no longer bear to listen to Meghan Pattyson's incessant, irritating laugh.") to thanks to Geno Auriemma for giving the state such a treasure. Sometimes the comments are very specific: "My sister had plantar fasciitis . . ." started one note, concerning former player Morgan Valley's debilitating foot condition. The letter finished with a prescription for a cure.

Other times the e-mails are so basic as to be hard to believe. "What does 'crashing the boards' mean?" Or "What is it to be 'in the post'?" These questions are usually from the considerable number of older women in the audience, the same fans who are asking Unger in April to let them know the schedule for the coming season so that they can plan their trips to Florida around the televised games. Many just want her to tell the coach "we love him," and more often than not, the communications have little to do with basketball. Here are some samples:

"I have been a women's fan and ticket holder since 1990 . . . love all the excitement, joy, and pride your teams have brought to this state (but) could you please tell Brittany Hunter, I would wear some sensible shoes instead of wearing those really high heels. They can't be good for the knee." (Hunter, a transfer from Duke, given to wearing pink and black spike heels, was on the bench all last season recuperating from a knee injury and sitting out the NCAA-required year for transfers.)

"I have noticed that a lot of the players chew gum whilst playing. I was taught, growing up, not to run around with anything in your mouth as it could prove to be hazardous (choking or asphyxiation could occur especially when playing so hard). Is this the kind of message we want to send to young viewers?"

"Who winds Diana's bun?" (The viewer is referring to the lump of hair that sat on the back of Diana Taurasi's head for four years. The answer, by the way: She winds it herself.)

"What are Tonya (Cardoza) and Jamelle (Elliott) always writing down on the sidelines?" (The assistant coaches keep track of players' individual stats—rebounds, shots, turnovers—as well as time-outs, fouls, and the like.)

America—the land of the quick judgment and the First Amendment. Ain't it grand?

love is college basketball because of the excitement "that has to do with the proximity of the crowd sitting right on top of you." In this regard, Gampel Pavilion, where the first-level fans are just feet away from the hardwood, is ideal, he said. His only regret about the women's fans, markedly different than those who attend the men's games, is that more students aren't involved.

"Spunky, can I get the away coach please?" Jensen commands into the headset, which matches those worn by the four CPTV cameramen who staff most games. In a flash the face of USF coach Jose Fernandez, his mouth a straight dark line across his face, appears on-screen as he paces in front of his bench. At this point in the game, UConn is against the ropes; nothing's falling and USF is making impossible shots. "USF is joining the Big East next season . . . " Picozzi reminds viewers who may be having difficulty keeping the team realignments straight. "Big East graphic," barks Mancini. In less than five seconds, thousands discover what the conference will look like a year hence (USF, Louisville, DePaul, Cincinnati, and Marquette in; Boston College out). A similar graphic is displayed during the Michigan State game, only this one shows how the Spartans had already beaten Boston College and Notre Dame, two Big East teams, before adding Connecticut to their list.

Even during the 20- and 30-point Connecticut blowouts (and there have been plenty of those over the years), the announcers know if they stop calling the game—if they miss a shot or a turnover—the CPTV switchboard and e-mail links will light up with angry viewers. "If they have a 20-point lead and I'm telling a story through a shot, we hear from them. They don't want to miss anything," says Pattyson-Cuomo. "We have to constantly be talking about the game," says Unger. "They want to see every inbound, every dribble . . . they don't want to see Sally Jones sitting in the audience even though I want people to see her holding up a CPTV sign for our fund-raisers. They don't want funky; they want meat and potatoes."

> Meanwhile, at the USF game, Barbara Turner has just stolen the ball and scored on a break. It is now 25–19, the enemy in charge, but the fans are on their feet as UConn starts one of its devastating runs to get back into the lead. "Charde Houston . . . scoring off the break," says one of the announcers. The replay shows the talented freshman streaking down court to stick it. "That'll get this crowd going," says Pattyson-Cuomo, as 10,000 people rise as one to their feet. "We finally have a game," Pattyson-Cuomo tells the truck during a time-out, while a CPTV promotion for a European Christmas concert is running. No doubt the thousands of viewers throughout the state are too busy to notice, breathing a sigh of relief that "their girls" have climbed back in it.

It's a mindset difficult to grasp beyond the state borders. Unger says at PBS development conferences, representatives of other stations in other states frequently look at her with amazement when they learn about the success of this phenomenon of televising women's basketball games. And then when she goes into the details of what it costs the station to have that privilege, balanced against the pledges and generally high profile it gives CPTV in the state, the already-stunned colleagues are even more shocked. A typical reaction: "You mean you pay *them* for the rights?" It's a big chunk of change for a public television station struggling to make it in the world of cable and network TV, but the returns to Connecticut Public Television from the UConn women's basketball program and all of its successes have and will continue to be immeasurable.

"On the whistle go for Battle," Jensen commands a cameraman. It is Senior Night 2005 — the last chance for the fans to see Ashley Battle, Jessica Moore, Ashley Valley, and Stacey Marron during the regular season at home. A player given to four years of inconsistency, Battle has shone all night with a career-high 23 points that put her over the 1,000 mark for her career. "Couldn't have scripted it better," Pattyson-Cuomo says with a laugh, during an interview with the quartet taped moments earlier while a plea for funds was running. Battle grins into the camera. Meanwhile, in the truck there is a rush to post the latest Big East standings: The season is winding down, and UConn is a game out of first behind Rutgers. "Just give the score of the Rutgers game verbally," Mancini begs Picozzi when there is a delay in putting the standings on the screen. As he is talking about the Rutgers victory over Boston College, the fonts pull it out and the standings flash. "Is everyone on the same page?" Mancini asks in a calm, but firm voice, her stopwatch an arm's length away. "10-9-8-7-6 . . . ," coordinating producer Anthony Meliso is counting down to the end of the live broadcast. "3-2-1 . . . ," Mancini picks up the count. Then, "We're clear." No one says, "It's a wrap"—that's apparently Hollywood stuff; instead

Pattyson-Cuomo thanks everyone "for putting up with me." She is hoarse from a bad cold and has been popping cough drops on the sidelines all night. No matter. The show must go on.

The Kid from the Crossroads

Like most tough New England Yankees, the residents of the tiny community of Epping, New Hampshire, have never been particularly overwhelmed by the fact that a superhero has lived in their midst. If Kerry Bascom was a nationally honored women's basketball player, well, that's just what Kerry does and does well.

In fact, Bascom, the UConn women's team's first-ever All-American, had a greater following in Connecticut, where she led the Huskies to their first Final Four, set a scoring record that would last for seven years, and still has the reputation of being among the best players to ever wear the blue and white. Her four years at Connecticut came during a time when the team was moving from the ranks of the losers (two winning seasons in thirteen) to the ranks of the winners where success in the Big East and at the national level started to become realities. In many ways her years represented the greatest transition period from the early years of head coach Geno Auriemma to the program of today.

In her own hometown of Epping (population 5,500), a cross-roads established in 1741 off Route 125 in southeastern New Hampshire, the only tangible reminder that she was a special athlete is the lone blue and white number 24 banner hanging in the Epping High School gym. No other number has ever been retired. The 2,000-plus points she scored as a star on the Blue Devils girls basketball team was surpassed a few years back—by a boy who had the advantage of the three-point shot.

UConn doesn't retire numbers as such, but when Nykesha Sales, who broke Bascom's scoring record in 1998—and still holds it—asked for number 24, she was told it was unavailable. (Instead, she reversed the number and wore 42 through her own illustrious career.) Sales's record-breaker (for 2,178 points) was the shot heard 'round the world, a set-up deal at Villanova when she hobbled onto the court in a foot cast for a free throw, her college career finished a month earlier when she ruptured her Achilles tendon. Bascom knew about the scheme (the two coaches had agreed to it days earlier) and, as could be expected, had no hard feelings about the event. "Why should it bother me?" she responds when asked about it. "That's what records are for."

After her collegiate playing days, Bascom became the first UConn player ever to play in Europe, for two years on club teams in Spain and France. (The WNBA had not yet formed.) Traveling helped fulfill her father David Bascom's suggestion in 1991 when she graduated from college that it was time for her to "spread her wings."

Eventually, however, that considerable wingspan brought her back to New Hampshire . . . 8 miles down the road from Epping to the larger community of Exeter with triple the population. There she works as a case manager for Community Partners Inc., overseeing some twenty or so emotionally and mentally disabled adults, a job that is every bit as rewarding as anything she did on the basketball court. She takes particular pride in her work with the Special Olympics, a pride based on a healthy respect for competition whether it is recognized by a fluttering blue ribbon pinned on a ten-year-old runner with Down syndrome or a glitzy silver trophy with her name and BIG EAST PLAYER OF THE YEAR engraved across the front in large block letters.

As she was growing up, Kerry and her boy pals shot hoops in the school yard. "I hung out with the guys and played pickup games with them," she said. Her family's backyard, which emptied out onto the baseball and softball fields down a gentle hill, was a gathering place for her friends.

"Every Saturday morning there was a knock on the door and some boys would be standing there," recalled David Bascom. "'Mr. Bascom, can Kerry come out and play?' they would ask me. Soccer, football, basketball, baseball you name it, she played it."

In high school she wanted to play baseball instead of softball, but even though her family appealed to state authorities, she was not allowed to play with the boy's team.

Kerry Bascom goes up for a shot.
University of Connecticut Division of Athletics

"I took the state to task on it," said David Bascom, "but they said 'no' because softball was available as an alternative." However, he successfully convinced officials to let her play in the all-boy Little League and the Pony League because baseball at this level was not an option for girls.

Soccer was a different story. As there was no girls' soccer team, Title IX, the landmark federal legislation that made an effort to equalize sports opportunities, dictated that she could play on the boys' team, which she did as the goalie.

She had to play on the girls' basketball teams, but even then exceptions were made for her dazzling abilities. Because Epping High School was in the small-school division (150 students), basketball coaches could draw from the middle school to fill out their rosters. So high school coach Ron Weitzell asked Kerry to join the team and in her first game with the junior varsity, she scored 25 points. At the time she was 6 feet tall and in the seventh grade. "She looked like a giant out there," her father said.

By grade eight, she was averaging 30 points a game for the JV. It was obvious that she was ready for bigger challenges. Once again Weitzell asked for and received an exception to state rules, this time to put her on the varsity. That decision was immediately validated: In her first game she scored 12 points in just four minutes off the bench.

She led Epping High School to a state championship in the small-school category during her sophomore year. Only because the second-best player was injured did they fail to repeat the following two years, having to settle for runner-up status. By this time, word had gotten out about this phenom from Epping, New Hampshire, and colleges were in hot pursuit of her. Her two major priorities were that she'd be close enough to home to see her mother, Eleanor Bascom, who had suffered from multiple sclerosis for a decade, and that she'd be guaranteed some playing time rather than just sit on the bench. After narrowing her final choices to Connecticut, Boston College, and Rutgers, she and her father visited all three campuses and then each drew up a list of pluses and minuses about the individual programs.

After the campus visits, B.C. and Rutgers continued their pursuit of the player, calling and writing Bascom as much as NCAA regulations allowed. But UConn head coach Geno Auriemma used a different approach. Taking heed of David Bascom's warning that Kerry is better left alone to make her decision, he kept in touch with the father instead, and finally on Christmas Day, she told Auriemma she would accept his offer. "I thought Geno would crawl through the phone and give her a big kiss," David Bascom recalled of the coach's reaction.

Several factors drove her to choose Connecticut: For one thing, it was less than a three-hour drive from Epping. Second, she felt she could make a major impact on turning things around, and she loved a challenge. But, perhaps, most important, the green hills of Storrs, where cows roam in the fields of what was once the Connecticut Agricultural College, reminded her of home. Her father agreed with the choice, and the following September she traded granite for nutmeg and headed two states south.

At first, the journey was tough. Her freshman year she struggled. By now 6'1", she was backup center behind Renee Najarian, a transfer student from South Carolina and at the time one of the best rebounders in the country. (Najarian's average of 10.1 boards a game in the two years she played still ties with that of Rebecca Lobo for a career high.) After her first year when the team went 17–11, Bascom used to hang around the basketball court practicing her shooting. One day, Auriemma saw her popping three-point shots, and based on what he saw, he hatched a plan that would turn her into one of the game's premier scorers. For Kerry Bascom, there was to be no R&R that summer.

After school was over in May, she went home to Epping, determined to return to Storrs in September a better long-range shooter. She was true to her word. She and her father convinced the Epping High School principal to give her a key to the gym, and every night, no matter how hot or tired they both were, the two of them let themselves into the school to practice. Every few feet along the three-point arc, they taped an X and then the daughter would start on her semicircle journey. She had to make 7 of 10 shots from each spot before she could move to the next, most nights taking as many as 500 shots. On unbearably hot evenings, they did the same thing on the outside court, but since it lacked a three-point line, they first had to spend time painting an arc. During the day she was involved in softball leagues and other sports, but no matter how tired she was, "she'd come home, take a shower, and we'd go up to the gym," her father said. Kerry, herself, recalled how sore her shoulders and elbows were each evening.

Auriemma's thinking on the matter was that if his 6'1" center could develop an outside shot, she'd be difficult to guard by even the best defenders. Did it work? The numbers tell the story. Her freshman year she was 0 for 3 from long range, averaging twenty minutes a game. Her sophomore season, when she started all twenty-nine games, the hard work began to pay off. She was confident in her three-point shot, took 126 of them, made 60, for 47.6 percent. Her junior and senior years, her three-point

Kerry Bascom's UConn Statistics

Games played:	120
Field goals:	803
Field goal average:	51.3 percent
3-point field goals:	161
3-point field-goal average:	39.5 percent
Free throws:	410
Free throw average:	79.6 percent
Rebounds:	915
Rebound average:	7.6
Assists:	221
Turnovers:	297
Steals:	127
Blocks:	27
Points:	2,177
Points per game:	18.1

shooting fell off about 10 percentage points, but the addition of sophomore sharpshooter Wendy Davis to the lineup allowed Bascom to play more of an inside-outside game, so she took fewer long-range shots (52 of 137). (Davis's record of 279 career three-pointers was finally broken in the 2003–04 season by Diana Taurasi, who finished her senior year with 318. Bascom's 161 are fifth all-time.)

In the meantime, other aspects of Bascom's game were improving. She was more fit, more consistent, and deadly from just about any place on the court. In four years she averaged 18.1

points a game (still the record for career average) and is among the top five players in most front-court offensive and defensive categories. "To me a great player is capable of doing anything on the court," Auriemma said of Bascom during a ceremony for one of her many honors. "Kerry is awfully close to that. She could be 2 inches taller or a little quicker—the great ones have all of that—but with her the biggest compliment is that she's taken what she's been given and gotten the most out of it. That's all you can ask of anyone."

As with most great players, as the stakes grew higher, Bascom elevated her game. Those who followed her career will never forget her performance against seventeenth-seeded Toledo, an aggressive, fearless team from the Mid-American Conference, in the second round of the 1991 NCAA tournament at Gampel Pavilion. Toledo had just knocked off number-six seed Rutgers, so confidence was brimming as they walked into Gampel, with its 4,000-plus screaming Husky fans—a healthy crowd in those days. During the regular season, number-three-seeded Connecticut (27–4) had gone 14–1 on that court.

Toledo started the game sluggishly; it appeared the Huskies would have it all their way. But the Rockets hung tough and, midway through the first half, fought back from an 11-point deficit to tie the score. For most of the rest of the game, they kept it close by packing the lane and forcing Bascom outside. In previous games leading up to the Toledo match, Bascom's three-point shot had deserted her, but this night, with a trip to the Sweet Sixteen on the line, she came up big. Moving around the three-point line, her sweat-soaked hair plastered to her face, her shirt out, she pumped in five of seven attempts as if it was just another hot August night at the Epping High School playground. But she had clearly saved the best for last (it was her final game at Gampel). With her team down 80–78, with 19 seconds left, Bascom inbounded the ball to guard Debbie Baer, who brought the ball up and passed it off to Orly Grossman, an Israeli who only stayed at UConn one year. Bascom, meanwhile, was driving to the basket. As the clock wound down, Grossman flipped her the ball, she made an impossible reverse layup, and drew a foul to boot. UConn was up 81–80, which was to be the final score. Toledo still had some fight left and managed to get three shots off, but each time they were tipped away by Bascom and forward Meghan Pattyson. Kerry finished with a total of 39 points, 16 of them in the final nine minutes. She also had 12 rebounds and 3 assists and played all but three minutes of the game. Afterward, Auriemma said Bascom's movement on the court made her impossible to guard. "When she's in that groove, you can't stop her."

The win earned Connecticut a trip to the Palestra in Auriemma's hometown of Philadelphia, where they knocked off two Atlantic Coast Conference powers in number-two-seed North Carolina State and number-five-seed Clemson to advance to the Huskies' first-ever Final Four. In three games (Connecticut had a bye in the first round) leading up to the national semifinal against Virginia, Bascom had 84 points and 23 rebounds and was named Final Eight tournament MVP.

Ranked number two in the NCAA tournament, Virginia, with an All-American point guard named Dawn Staley and the twin towers of Heidi and Heather Burge, lay waiting for the Huskies in New Orleans. Clearly the underdogs, Connecticut went into the weekend with the idea of having fun, playing loose, and getting as much out of the experience as possible. "I was part of a team that took one step at a time," Bascom recalled recently when asked about the experience in New Orleans, the same city where Connecticut won its third straight national championship in 2004. "New Orleans wasn't one moment . . . it was a lot of hard work from the field house to Gampel Pavilion. It was all pieces of a whole. That's what went into New Orleans."

Predictably UConn lost to Virginia 61–55. Bascom, saddled with three fouls early in the game, sat out much of the first half. Although she put together a mini-scoring run in the second half, she finished with only 14 points on six of fourteen chances. She didn't take one three-point shot; the defense of Virginia's Tonya Cardoza was like nothing she had ever seen. "She was pinned to me the entire game," Bascom said at the time. In an almost chilling foreshadowing of things to come, at one point when Cardoza stumbled toward the UConn bench, Auriemma playfully ushered her toward a seat with the Huskies. Three years later she was to join the team, this time as an assistant coach, which she is to this day. When she thinks back on that national semifinal, Cardoza says the one thing that stands out in her mind is how tough it was to guard the UConn center. "Guarding Kerry Bascom and keeping her off the boards wore me out," Cardoza said. She was still her team's high scorer with 16 points (Wendy Davis's 17 points led all shooters) although Connecticut's defense held the Cavaliers to 30 points below their season average of 91 a game. (It's possible the entire Virginia team was worn out by the semifinal. The next night they lost to Tennessee in the national finals. They had run out of gas.)

That same week in New Orleans, Bascom was named to the Kodak All-America team, the first of what would be many Connecticut players to receive the sport's highest distinction. After receiving the award, she said that she had told her dad years earlier she didn't like talking about herself, but this was one award she had set her sights on. "I think every kid in America that plays basketball wants this," she said. (She had already been Big East Player of the Year three straight times, a feat accomplished only once before—that by the great Shelley Pennefather of Villanova from 1984 to 1986.) And then she said something else, a simple statement that put the glow of her collegiate career in an even greater light. "This award is for my mom," she added, with the slight lisp that is still part of her speech. "She always told me to work hard, and I think I have done that."

Though Bascom is rarely emotional or self-absorbed, this brief moment was reminiscent of that chilly night in December 1989, after the first semester of her junior year, when a friend, an Epping policewoman, showed up at a game unexpectedly. It was a Wednesday night, and the team was still playing to fewer than 200 fans in the old field house. "As we warmed up I saw her in the stands in her uniform," Bascom recalled. "I thought 'That's weird. She has to be at work early tomorrow.'"

After the game, in the "shoebox" of a locker room, the door opened and Auriemma and the policewoman suddenly appeared. "You need to call your dad," Auriemma told Bascom, who by that time was racing toward his office. Over the phone, her father told her she needed to come home—that her mother was very sick.

When she got home, her mother was in the intensive care unit at a hospital in Exeter. Kerry, her father, and her paternal grandmother sat by her bedside in eight-hour shifts as the woman slowly faded away. A few weeks earlier, Eleanor Bascom had opted to have an experimental procedure that was believed could help late-stage MS victims. At the time 70 percent of those who

Kerry Bascom, surrounded by trophies and symbols of her playing days.
University of Connecticut Division of Athletics

had the procedure improved, 20 percent stayed the same, and 10 percent died. Eleanor, then forty, had told her husband, "David, I'm going to do it." When he played devil's advocate and asked her why, she repeated the statistics and said, "It's worth the try." But three days after she had the procedure, she grew very ill. On December 14, 1989, she died, but not before, between pain and medications, she extracted a promise from her oldest daughter to return to school and complete her education. "At first I didn't want to go back," Kerry recalled. There was the matter of her two younger sisters, Kelly and Kiley, and the fourth member of the family, as well. "She wanted to stay home and take care of dad," said David Bascom. "We had a talk, I reminded her of her promise to her mother and that I had promised her that all three of her daughters would have a college education." Both promises were met: Kelly, three years younger than Kerry, is a teacher, and Kiley, nine years younger, is pursuing a nursing degree. A decade ago David Bascom remarried and once again there is a complete family on Cate Street. Ironically, the woman he married is the mother of Kerry's husband, Shawn Poloquin. Epping, New Hampshire, *is* a small community.

And so when the new semester began in January 1990, Kerry Bascom was back in Storrs, back in class, and back on the basketball court. She hadn't missed that many games because the team took a break for finals and the holidays. "I don't really remember much about my junior year," she said. "At least basketball gave me something to do."

Her dad had a stronger opinion. "It was the best thing in the world for her at the time," he said. He continued making the round-trip to and from Epping for all home games, often with his two other daughters in tow. In December 1991 she fulfilled her deathbed promise to her mother and graduated with a degree in sociology. Europe was next, and then she became an assistant basketball coach at the University of New Hampshire in nearby Durham. That job kept her in touch with the game that had defined her life, but after five years she decided it was time to be closer to Epping and her family, so she left Durham and returned home.

These days she rarely picks up a basketball. For a while she played in a women's league in Portsmouth but was so superior to the other players, she found herself inhibiting her play so she wouldn't physically injure them. Since it was not her style to hold back on anything, she quit the league. These days it's Wiffle ball or a pickup softball game or Special Olympics or trips to the dog track with her dad.

"Ever since 1991, I'm a nobody. And that's fine with me," she says. The kid from the New Hampshire crossroads a nobody? Kerry Bascom, the player who was in on the ground floor of a program that would come to dominate the sport, a nobody? Only in her own mind does that label have any validity. For true Husky fans, she'll always be part of their memories of the dawn of a great tradition.

Those Husky Fans

Nothing can stop them: not distance, blizzards, infirmity. They have traveled thousands of miles and forked up thousands of dollars to see these tall athletic women whom they treat as members of the family. They are truly the UConn women's basketball team's sixth men. They are the fans.

Take the trials and tribulations of one Harold Drayton, a man in his seventies from Bridgeport. His fanaticism may be extreme, but he is representative of the way the citizens of this small, densely populated state, wedged between the pro sports meccas of Boston and New York, have embraced the UConn women as "their girls."

Harold Drayton does not drive. Years ago, this retired owner of a dry cleaning business said that too many accidents and too costly insurance forced him to "turn in my plates." Living in Bridgeport doesn't pose too many problems: There is public transportation or he can walk to nearby amenities or get others to drive him. But without a license how do you get to Hartford (60 miles away) or Storrs (84 miles)—sometimes twice a week—to see your favorite team do their traveling, 94 feet up and down the court, over and over again, to win yet another game?

There's no question he'll go, but that decision has come at a price for Harold Drayton.

Here's a typical forty-eight hours in the life of Harold Drayton as he travels to and from his home in Bridgeport to the pastureland of the University of Connecticut. Let's say the game is Sunday afternoon at 2:00. Whereas students may roll out of bed and over to Gampel, or those coming by car hop into their vehicles at 12:30 P.M. and are there by the time the doors open at 1:00 P.M., Harold Drayton greets the paper boy at 6:30 in the morning when he must leave his home for the 2:00 P.M. rendezvous. His first step is a taxi to the Greyhound bus station (city buses aren't operating that early on Sunday). From there, he catches an early morning bus to Hartford, which runs him $30 not including the cab ride. Once in Hartford he catches another bus to Storrs, which will cost him another $17 round-trip. (When the team plays at the Hartford Civic Center, which they do for half of their schedule, Drayton can stay in Hartford, walk to the Civic Center, and save himself a few dollars.)

Once in Storrs, the bus drops him off at the corner of Hill-side and Alumni Roads. He walks a few yards to Gampel Pavilion and then climbs to the upper reaches of the arena to take his regular reserved seat. Finally Drayton can relax for a few hours watching his team manhandle their latest victims. (If he dozes off during a 30-point blowout, who could blame him? But he's too great a fan to fall asleep on the job.) When the game ends about 5:00 P.M.—usually it's already dark and cold—he may or may not be able to catch a bus back to Hartford and then home, depending on how late it lasts. On weeknights, when games start at 7:30 P.M., he has no choice but to make overnight arrangements in the area.

In the past, he would call a taxi to drive him 12 miles south to the Best Western Motel ($95 a night) on the outskirts of Willi-mantic. For the past three years, however, he has been able to stay overnight on campus at the newly constructed Nathan Hale Inn, a comfortable upscale lodging but not that easy on the wallet (single rooms run $130 a night). Regardless of where he stays, the next morning Drayton must retrace his steps to Bridgeport, which means another bus to Hartford and then another from Hartford to home. The totals in time and money to see the game: more than $200 and at least twenty-four hours, but for Harold Drayton, the experience, as the ad says, is priceless.

As it is for the thousands of fans across Connecticut for whom life begins each year on Super Sunday, the mid-October, circus-like free show and scrimmage to introduce the latest crop of Huskies and to reintroduce the veterans to their adoring public. With the arena darkened, the players and coaches come out one by one through a fake ring of fire to high-pitched, energetic music by the pep band. Some dance like they're going clubbin', others walk casually as if stepping up to the free throw line, still others cheer and point to the crowd, which greets them with roars of approval. It's a family show for the hundreds of mothers, fathers, and young kids who make up the overwhelming percentage of fans each game.

After the show, long tables are set up on the Gampel Pavilion concourse where hundreds of people—mostly young girls and their curious parents—line up ten and twelve deep for autographs. In fact autograph seekers follow these women everywhere. Diana Taurasi, (2000–2004) became a celebrity during her years at UConn. She recalled countless incidents of being mobbed in shopping malls, at restaurants, on beaches thousands of miles away when she was vacationing in Mexico. (In her senior year, the adoration had reached such a pitch that she often found it easier to stay home.) E-mails pour into the players' UConn addresses—they are publicly listed on the university Web site— too many to begin to handle. When Connecticut won the 2003 national championship behind the expert ballhandling of junior Maria Conlon (no turnovers in thirty-nine minutes), thousands turned out on the green in her hometown of Derby (population 12,000), about an hour away from Storrs, for speeches and other ceremonies on Maria Conlon Day.

If the team loses, a pall settles over the state. Newspaper story after story analyzes what's "wrong" with the women. Editorials in major state newspapers try to cheer up the depressed population. UConn head coach Geno Auriemma, whose UConn e-mail address is also public, receives dozens of suggestions for righting

Husky fans at a 1995 women's basketball game against Tennessee.
University of Connecticut Division of Athletics

the ship: bench this one, move this player to this spot. Sometimes Tennessee fans write to chide him. He usually ignores the e-mails but occasionally, if someone has really annoyed him, will shoot back a caustic answer with the words *five national championships* embedded somewhere in the note.

The UConn Athletic Department is scrupulous about the popular autograph signings by athletes at public places, such as shopping malls. Some events have been canceled as too exploitative. On the rare occasions the women are permitted to do it, such as for charity, fans line up hours in advance to have ten seconds with the players as they sign posters, hats, magazine covers, photos, sneakers, basketballs—anything that will take a Sharpie.

■ ■ ■

The Huskies actually have two home courts (both have been sold out for years): Gampel Pavilion, which opened in January 1990 and expanded from 8,000 to 10,167 seats several years ago; and the Hartford Civic Center, which holds 16,294. In recent years, following in the footsteps of the men's program, the women have increased the number of games at the Civic Center so it now constitutes 50 percent of the home schedule. The big nonconference games, against Tennessee and Duke, for example, are usually in the city because more fans can see them. In fact, both UConn teams have kept the Civic Center, and many of the surrounding bars and restaurants, in business, although a recent renovation project to replace the center's defunct shopping mall with luxury apartments and businesses is hoped by city officials to bring people back downtown. During the construction, the arena remained standing and patrons picked their way through the site to get inside for the games.

The Glory That Is Home

The UConn women's team splits its home schedule between Gampel Pavilion, a space-age-like dome on the rural Storrs campus, and the Hartford Civic Center, a classic downtown arena surrounded by city streets.

Based on attendance and records, the team draws equally well in both places and plays equally well in the city and the country. Since 1999 the Huskies have played every regular-season home game in the two venues before sellout crowds. Through the 2004–05 season, they were second in overall attendance only to Tennessee, which has played in the 24,525-seat Thompson Boling Arena since the 1987 season. Five times in the ten years since the 1994–95 season, Connecticut has surpassed its SEC rival in yearly attendance, usually hovering around the 200,000 mark, depending on the Gampel–Civic Center split.

By the end of the 2004–05 regular season, more than two million fans had passed through the Gampel Pavilion and Hartford Civic Center turnstiles. The home records are staggering. Until they lost to Notre Dame on January 30, 2005, UConn had won fifty-one straight games at Gampel. From their first game there (January 31, 1990) through the 2004–05 season, their cumulative regular-and-postseason record was 210–16. The cumulative Civic Center record, dating back to 1980 when they played the first of a double-header with the men's team (they played only nine games in Hartford from 1980 to 1990), is 54–8.

Typically the first home game each season begins with the raising of a banner with thousands on their feet for several minutes while the forlorn players on the opposing team's bench sit motionless, wondering if they'll be the first victim in the Huskies' latest march to March Madness success. The home regular season typically ends with fans dabbing their eyes with tissues, as they bid farewell to the seniors. In the case of Svetlana Abrosimova, who came to this country from her native St. Petersburg, Russia, at seventeen years old, barely able to speak English, the farewell was particularly poignant. A few days before the ceremony, her parents had ventured out of Russia for the first time in their lives. When they had booked the journey, they intended to see Svet's final regular-season games as a U.S. college student and the Big East tournament. But a foot injury had abruptly ended her college career. (Early on, fans took to Abrosimova with such passion that they had grey shirts made up with the words SVET SHIRT printed on them.) Senior night, with her mother on one arm, her father on the other, she hobbled to center court on crutches to receive a standing ovation. There wasn't a dry eye in the house.

In past eras particular sections of Gampel have become unofficial headquarters of rooting sections for a specific player. Anyone who has frequented the games for the past fifteen years will remember vividly the cries of "Berube," as they thundered through the upper regions, whenever Massachusetts native Carla Berube came off the bench during the mid-1990s.

For years, an elderly woman sat behind the Husky basket three or four rows from the floor (for only part of the season because she winters in Florida). She had been dubbed "the sign lady" by the media for holding up and twisting around to show the crowd large cardboard placards with hand-written puns about the drubbing the opposing team was facing. WE'LL SHOOT DOWN THE EAGLES (Boston College) and KNIGHT, KNIGHT RUTGERS (they are the Scarlet Knights) are samples of her humor. She sits at the end of a row of ten-year-old girls with blue Husky paws tattooed on their cheeks, staring wide-eyed and worshipful as the events unfold on the court. If they're lucky, they may be plucked out of the stands by the UConn marketing interns to participate in one of the time-outs when two kids put on oversized Husky uniforms and sneakers, clomp down the court, and try to make a basket before the other.

In recent years a student has appeared behind the visitors' basket with half his face painted white, half blue. He is silent through most of the game—and particularly noticeable at the tip-off and during free throws when he stands solemnly, his arms thrust straight out as if he's in a semi-worshipful pose. Not a lot of students attend the games, although the players' friends are frequently there, with signs for their pals.

In the early years of the team's success, fans applauded every UConn basket or rebound or steal with great fervor; but as they have become more savvy (and more sure of victories), they tend to save their enthusiasm for close games, or to pick up the team in the rare instance that they fall behind at home. When the game is a blowout, some fans leave long before the final seconds tick off the clock. At the start of the 2004 season, when the Huskies were struggling against the University of South Florida, Auriemma lashed out at the crowd saying they had given up on the women too early in the game. His comments drew imme-diate responses from fans, who said he had insulted them in the heat of the moment; some, however, continued their adoration of

Husky fans come in all different shapes, sizes, and colors.
University of Connecticut Division of Athletics

the coach who has brought so much glory to the program (and by association, to them).

Other times, the fans can turn things around. If they perceive that their girls are getting bad calls, for example, spectators are all over the refs. If a game's a blowout, fans boo opposing coaches who order players to foul the Huskies, even though they're hopelessly behind and the fouls only delay the inevitable. The fans, the large majority of them female, also reveal their humanity time and time again—applauding an injured player on the opposing team or, in some cases, good basketball no matter who the perpetrator. But they can hold grudges, such as the disdain in which they held Tennessee's tough All-American Semeka Randall after she decked Svetlana Abrosimova during a struggle for the ball in Knoxville. (She was henceforth known as "Boo" even at home.) A year earlier Randall had enraged UConn fans when she hit an off-balance prayer at the buzzer to give Tennessee a 1-point victory at Gampel. Fans never let Randall forget the Abrosimova incident and booed her every time they laid eyes on her—even in 2004, years after she had graduated, when she returned as an assistant coach with Michigan State. "Do they still hate me?" she joked at the time.

■ ■ ■

Connecticut weather can be pretty raw at the end of March and in early April, but poor weather has never affected the crowds that turn out at Bradley Airport in Windsor Locks when the plane carrying a victorious UConn national championship team touches down. After the first NCAA championship (Minneapolis 1995), thousands of people lined the bus route from Windsor Locks to Storrs. Signs hung from bridges and over stop signs; billboards proclaimed them champions; Husky banners flew in front yards as the team bus slowly made its way down highways and backcountry roads, players smiling and waving from the windows. In 2000, when a victorious team returned from winning a championship in Philadelphia, they were greeted by the governor who had a bouquet of roses for each player. He had also ordered the words UCONN WOMEN, 2000 NATIONAL CHAMPIONSHIP to flash on electronic signs normally warning motorists of construction and traffic problems.

Road games often become home games for the Huskies thanks to the caravan of buses that take Connecticut fans up and down the East Coast to follow the team. Boston College, which was turning into a legitimate rival (they beat UConn in the 2004 Big East semifinals in Hartford), even went so far as to limit the number of tickets that could be sold to people from Connecticut in hopes of neutralizing the support. Other teams offer special deals to try to pack the house with their fans: $1 tickets for adults, children free; everybody free—that type of thing. Many teams, especially Big East squads with small followings, have set attendance records on the days the Huskies came to town.

Months before the NCAA tournaments, local travel agents are working on packages that include air fare, hotels, and tickets to the Final Four. And as soon as the NCAA opens the lottery for the next year's Final Four, applications from Connecticut flood in. Many are disappointed as the tickets are usually divvied up so that each school gets the same amount. That, however, doesn't guarantee neutral houses, as two-thirds of the seats are usually filled with either Connecticut or Tennessee fans who snap up extra tickets on eBay or from scalpers. For big games in Hartford or Storrs (against, say, Rutgers, Tennessee, or Duke), scalpers can get up to $500 a ticket.

"I think we are the only team in the country that has never had an away game," associate head coach Chris Dailey once remarked. "Everywhere we go, our fans are there. They put our program at another level."

The program really did reach another level—from solid conference winners to national powers—in 1995 when their 35–0 season was capped off with the national championship victory in Minneapolis. The point guard at the time was junior Jen Rizzotti, whose 1992–93 freshman year was a struggle—the team went 18–11, with a loss in the first round of the NCAA tournament. In the early 1990s, 3,000 fans at most would show up for games—so few, in fact, it was possible for the players to come out into the Gampel stands to meet with their family and friends after a game.

During Rizzotti's sophomore year, however, things started to change. The team went 30–3, were Big East regular-season and tournament champs, and made it to the NCAA Final Eight before losing to North Carolina, which went on to win the NCAA title that year. Seizing the moment, then women's sports information director Barb Kowal aggressively and intelligently started marketing the team, and Gampel began filling up as women's basketball became a force in a state desperate for a winning sport. The crowds grew: 4,000, 5,000, finally the first sellout on February 20, 1993, when the Huskies lost 68–54 to defending national champion Stanford before a national television audience. Again families and older fans constituted most of the crowd.

Since a December 1997 game against Rutgers, Gampel has been sold out for every women's game. The crowds have also changed postgame routines. No longer could the players mingle freely in the stands. The autograph seekers and well-wishers had become too aggressive, and the players' families and friends had to go to the locker room for personal meetings with the players after the games.

Rizzotti will never forget those years that she was part of the explosion in popularity. "I remember that feeling of growth . . . of the building being full every time my junior year. Selling out every game. There is probably not a better feeling in the world than running out of that tunnel to the UConn fight song to a sellout," she said.

The greatest growth in fans occurred during Rizzotti's era, as did the dramatic increase in media coverage as more and more

Jen Rizzotti waves to the crowds during the 1995 national championship parade in Hartford. *University of Connecticut Division of Athletics*

Connecticut sports editors started to take notice of the emerging success story in Storrs. Kowal made sure that small daily newspapers got a steady stream of reports on players from their communities. She worked tirelessly to arrange phone interviews with hometown papers and television and radio stations, and soon the message of UConn women's basketball was being carried throughout the Northeast. She also exploited Auriemma's wit and ease with language, making sure he networked with UConn football and men's basketball beat writers during halftimes of their games so they could interview him for features. Today the women's team is covered by state sportswriters in greater numbers than any other women's team (professional or otherwise) in the country. (Tennessee, for example, has only one full-time beat reporter following them.) More than a dozen writers cover every home game, and about half as many travel with the team. At tournament time, the number of print journalists can triple, and the state's four major television networks send reporters and camera crews on the road for daily coverage.

In March 2004, *60 Minutes* did a special segment on the UConn women (Morley Safer was on the sidelines for a few games); the *New Yorker* magazine, normally home to Philip Roth, Roger Angell, and Seymour Hersh, did a lengthy profile on Taurasi; *Sports Illustrated* has featured the women as the cover story several times; and at least one slice-of-life book that followed the team through a season has been written. Rizzotti does television ads for a well-known Honda dealer in Eastern Connecticut, and Rebecca Lobo and others, including Meghan Pattyson, have parlayed their playing careers into successful careers as basketball television commentators.

The Co-Op: Barking Up the Right Tree

In a brilliant marketing move, the UConn Co-Op bookstore moved three and a half years ago from its former location near the Homer Babbidge Jr. Library in the heart of campus to a new two-story building across the street from Gampel Pavilion. The new store, which cost $21 million, opened in January 2002 with a first-floor Husky Shop, where racks of sweatshirts and warm-ups and counters of water bottles, mugs, watches, and just about anything large enough to take the UConn logo and a picture of the mascot, take up nearly half of the space. The Co-Op has probably recouped most of its construction costs through the tons of Husky merchandise that fans gobble up before and after the games. (It remains open well into the night for just that purpose.) Before a women's game, the aisles are packed with grandparents, parents, and their kids sifting through the merchandise. The most popular merchandise is championship clothing that re-creates the brackets and final scores, leading up to another successful Big East or national championship. At retail stores across Connecticut, there are (unlicensed) variations of championship merchandise: "UConn where men are men and women are

As the team continued to improve, increasing numbers of writers started showing up at practice to do game advances and features about players. By the time Rebecca Lobo arrived in the fall of 1991, Kowal could ease up on the arm twisting. Lobo was every parent's dream daughter—a straight-A student, well-spoken, attractive, witty—so she was an easy sell to the press. Kowal was also in relentless pursuit of the *New York Times* college basketball writer. Her work finally paid off when in 1995 champions" (until 2004 when both basketball teams brought trophies to eastern Connecticut), "64 ways to make a dream: only one to make a champion," and the like are popular, too.

Bill Simpson, who has been general manager of the Co-Op for more than twenty years, said on a day-to-day basis, the women's basketball merchandise outsells the men three to one. But after they won the national championship in 1999 and 2004, the men's merchandise was a bigger seller. The men's fans are more "corporate," Simpson said. The women's fans buy tickets in bunches, so some games they may send grandma, other games mom, and always the kids. Introducing children into the mix has boosted sales of women's merchandise tremendously, and these are fans who will outgrow a T-shirt and move up to the next size, so the market is guaranteed for years. Although he didn't provide actual sales figures, Simpson said counting the on-site, Web site, and outlet sales (the merchandise is available at Rentschler Field in East Hartford where the football team plays, in corner booths at Gampel during games, and at other select sites), sales are in the millions each year. Next to textbooks, basketball merchandise is the Co-Op's biggest moneymaker.

he wrote a comprehensive feature article on Lobo, Rizzotti, and the rest of the team as they headed into the final stages of their undefeated season. "Basically it all comes down to persuasion first, then building relationships, hustling to get all the pertinent information to the reporters, and letting them [the players] be themselves and tell their stories," Kowal said of that early success.

During the Lobo years, a new voice for the fans emerged in the form of The Husky Boneyard, an Internet bulletin board established by a couple of UConn fans for their friends. At first created primarily to talk about UConn men's basketball, it has grown from its narrow beginnings into a national Web site with six individual bulletin boards representing several Connecticut sports. During the school year, it's estimated the various sites get some 50,000 visitors a month (soccer, men's and women's basketball, football) but the women's basketball site is by far the most popular with nearly half of the visitors headed there, according to informal surveys. Often, newspaper articles by the beat writers are downloaded onto the site, and frequently they touch off heated debates. There's gossip about recruits (who's getting whom), reports of former Connecticut players in the WNBA, and other stuff to stir up the fans.

Nancy Pfaff of Wallingford, Connecticut, just north of New Haven, is one of the movers and shakers behind the Boneyard. Other teams have Web sites (Tennessee, for example, has The Summitt), but not to the extent of the UConn site. And the Boneyard interest doesn't end with graduation. "Once they've played at UConn, we follow them forever," said Pfaff, whose Web name Husky Nan is often attached to pregame analyses, game stories, and postgame reactions as if she was a beat writer for a major state newspaper.

She said the people monitoring the messages are careful to draw the line between legitimate, public news about the players and mean-spirited or otherwise "creepy" information that someone may want to post. She has detected stalkers trying to find out where to find players, and they have been banned from the site. "We don't need to know about a player's personal life unless there has been an article in the newspaper," she said. For example, "if there's an article about Sue Bird's latest boyfriend that's been in the New York papers, the Boneyard may pick it up, but if someone tries to post a message that they saw her talking to a guy in a restaurant, it would be denied."

Her attitude toward the young athletes whom she follows from high school, to college, and then to professional life reflects that of thousands like her: "We really don't think of them as UConn players or basketball players," she said. "To us, they are just our girls."

Shea Ralph: Never Say Die

One night as she was watching a WNBA game on television, Marsha Lake wondered how it was that Rebekkah Brunson, a solid, but inconsistent player when she was at Georgetown University, was earning thousands of dollars in the sport she loved, while her daughter, who had always had the better of Brunson and her Georgetown team, was an assistant college coach trying to help rebuild a losing program.

"Sometimes life isn't fair," Lake said. Sometimes clichés are the best way to express the truth.

Life hasn't been fair to Lake's daughter, Shea Ralph, or to Ralph's two damaged knees. Five times, three of them at the University of Connecticut and twice as a pro, she has suffered torn anterior cruciate ligaments (ACLs), injuries that cut short promising collegiate and professional basketball careers with the suddenness of a snap of a twig.

Four times she went through painful operations, long, tedious rehabs, and trying tests of will and endurance to work her way back onto the court.

The fifth time she ripped up her knee while playing winter ball with the now defunct Springfield (Massachusetts) Spirit. Her surgeon warned her that if she insisted on playing again, there was a good chance that by the time she was forty, the best case scenario was that she'd have two knee replacements, and the worst case, she'd be in a wheelchair.

At that time she was twenty-four. And so she quit playing.

For the first time in her life, she had to rein in her passion for the game that had made her a hometown hero first in Fayetteville, North Carolina, then a statewide hero when she played at the University of Connecticut, and finally a national hero when she gallantly tried to continue her career as a member of the Utah Starzz.

Even watching basketball being played by others was bringing pain into her life, pain far worse than that from her knee injuries. "I was upset, disappointed, and devastated that I

couldn't play any more," she recalls now. So she set about rein-
venting herself.

"I knew that I was better at things than just one thing," she
says, the Southern accent still dominant despite years of living in
the North. She got a job in the Hartford, Connecticut, school
system, motivating kids and doing special projects. Luck was to
be against her in that venture as well, when the funds for her
position were not budgeted for a second year.

Eventually her anger and frustration at basketball subsided,
and when the dust cleared, she still felt a passion for the game. "I
knew I could still be part of it and that I could make a difference,
even if I'm not out on the court playing," she said. And so in the
early summer of 2003, she entered a new phase of her life,
accepting a job as an assistant women's basketball coach at the
University of Pittsburgh, a Big East school that would put her on
the opposing bench when they played Connecticut each season.

"When she finally told me 'I think I want to coach,' I said,
'Hello, I've been telling you this for eight years,'" said Marsha Lake.
"And she loves it; she scrimmages with the players, she still exer-
cises even though she may not be able to walk for two days after-
wards, and she's found a place and what she needed at the time."

Her college coach, Geno Auriemma, was surprised when
Ralph entered coaching. "I never thought she'd have the
patience and disposition to be around people who didn't understand what she's about," Auriemma said. But, he knew as Ralph
knew, coaching was a way to stay in the game.

At Pitt her name opens doors in recruiting. Head coach
Agnus Berenato, entering her third year after fourteen years as
head coach at Georgia Tech, said that when the coaches visit
recruits, the neighbors often slip into the girls' living rooms and

ask Ralph for her signature on *Sports Illustrated* covers, UConn championship T-shirts, and other paraphernalia.

Like others who have gotten to know Ralph, Berenato most admires her heart. "She can't run, she can't jump, she has her knees all taped up, and she still beats my team five on one," the coach said. She said Ralph is like a sponge: She wants to learn and takes in everything she's taught. "We're educators. Sure, we teach the kids the pick and roll, we teach them to square up before they shoot, but it's also about how they walk through a lobby, how they greet people,"—in short, about being a role model. Shea Ralph fits the mold.

For Ralph, losing games has been difficult to cope with. But Ralph knows that even though her team lacks the skills and talent of the Huskies, she can still teach them the intangibles that go into winning—qualities that have been key to her makeup since the first day she picked up a ball.

Shea Ralph was never the quickest or strongest player, but she worked harder than anyone else, throwing herself on the floor for a loose ball, worming her way free to drain a three, inching her way sideways along the baseline to make an awkward lopsided layup even though her slight 6-foot frame was surrounded by far taller defenders.

She doesn't have any of her UConn trophies in her Pitt office (her mother has them all); that was another time and Pitt's a different place. "I want to make it clear that this is not Connecticut. I don't want to set that standard for these kids. They have to feel good about themselves. But I can create that atmosphere so these players can experience in their own way what I experienced."

She hopes to be a head coach someday, but now she knows she has a lot to learn. If she has to work eighteen hours a day and is the least experienced in the women's basketball office, well that's just the way it is "when you're trying to work your way up," says her mother.

Although she's in her early fifties, Ralph's mother, Marsha Lake, is still working her way up the ladder, completing work toward a doctorate in math education at the Florida Institute of Technology. She also teaches part-time at Brevard Community College in Titusville, not far from Cocoa Beach where she lives with her third husband, Roy Lake. He renewed their high school romance after he saw Shea Ralph on television in a UConn game, learned from the announcers she was from Fayetteville, and said to himself "that girl looks like Marsha Mann." Marsha was single at the time. A first marriage to Shea's natural father didn't work out, nor did her marriage to Bob Ralph, who adopted Shea and gave her a second daughter, Ryan, who is a programmer for a small Methodist college near Fayetteville. But this union with Roy Lake, she says, has made her happier than she's ever been in her life.

In this family the apple doesn't fall far from the tree. Shea Ralph has always needed something to reach for, and if things got in the way, well, she'd just try harder to make it work.

Through all of the injuries, there was never a public moment when she dared to ask, "Why me?" or thought about quitting until her orthopedic surgeon gave her the grim prognosis.

"Self-pity?" she responds to a questioner. "That's not my style. I wasn't brought up to think that way, and a lot of that has to do with the values that my mom gave me. When you get knocked down, you brush it off and get up. If you start having self-pity, you miss things in life. And things aren't going to pass me by."

For Shea Ralph everything has always been in fast-forward, whether that was being voted the national player of the year her junior year at UConn or killing herself in the weight room when her knee was aching, a biology test was facing her, and there was a foot of snow at the gym door.

"It really is paradise up there," Ralph said of her five years in Storrs, years that were as much about pain and frustration as about playing and winning. "The camaraderie, the family. I see it now especially being part of a different team."

She arrived in Storrs (20,000) from Fayetteville (130,000), an ambitious highly recruited freshman from a community where her name had been a household word since she was eleven years old and excelling at three sports. Her mother had been an All-America basketball player at North Carolina, so of course the Tar Heels were in hot pursuit, as was Tennessee (her mother was friends with Lady Vol head coach Pat Summitt). But Ralph felt at home in Connecticut. She had also decided that maybe it was time to leave the comfort zone and "test myself with athletics, academics, people, and the world."

The first glow of excitement of finally being out on her own quickly faded. Within two weeks of the start of school, she wanted to go back home where the topic of conversation on everyone's lips was either the upcoming Friday night high-school football game or the exciting blonde female athlete at Terry Sanford High School. In college, fantasy and reality often clashed. "All I heard when I was growing up was 'you're so great,'" she said. Instead, all she was hearing was the angry bark of Geno Auriemma telling her to work harder, to pass the ball once in a while, to pay attention to him if she wanted to improve. But despite the initial depression at being away from home, Ralph made an immediate impact and was named national freshman of the year by most voting groups. She was Big East rookie of the year as well. And then tragedy struck—at the end of her freshman season when she was leading the fast break during a first-round NCAA tournament game against Lehigh. The break ended with Ralph on the floor writhing in pain and a sophomore year as a medical redshirt, trying to work her way back onto the court.

Her second year of playing she played thirty games, led the team in scoring (16.8 points a game), and was second in steals with 69. She was named an honorable AP All-American and 1999 Big East tournament MVP. Everything pointed to the stardom that was to come.

And this is exactly what transpired the next season (her junior year), which was hands down her healthiest and most accomplished. That year (1999–2000) she and junior Svetlana Abrosimova led the Huskies (37–1) to their second NCAA national championship (both were Kodak All-Americans that year), and the highest national honors came her way, including the Honda Award as the nation's best collegiate basketball player. She started all thirty-seven games and led Connecticut in scoring (14.3 points a game), assists (181), and steals (95). She ranks seventh in career scoring (1,678), eighth in assists (456), and fifth in steals (252) on Connecticut career lists.

Coming off such a strong junior year, Ralph was urged by many to forgo her final year of eligibility and enter the WNBA draft, where she probably would have been among the top three picks. But Ralph had made a promise to an incoming freshman by the name of Diana Taurasi (who was ultimately to pass her in career points and steals) that she'd play one more year so they

Shea Ralph's UConn Statistics

Games played:	128
Field goals:	562
Field goal average:	57.9 percent
3-point field goals:	81
3-point field-goal average:	36.3 percent
Free throws:	473
Free throw average:	81.4 percent
Rebounds:	510
Rebound average:	4.0
Assists:	456
Turnovers:	290
Steals:	252
Points:	1,678
Points per game:	13.1

could share the backcourt. If nothing else Shea Ralph is true to her word and passionate about her commitments.

Her senior-year numbers were well off the mark: 9.7 points a game, 122 assists, 53 steals, and the best postseason honor she could muster was Second Team All-Big East. It's a year she considers the lowest point in her five at UConn. "I disappointed my teammates and my coach, but I was probably more disappointed in myself than they were in me," she said.

She met with Auriemma frequently about her uncharacteristic lack of energy. "He'd ask me, 'What's going on? You don't have that same fire in your eyes.'" It was a question for which she either had no answer or lots of them: Burnout? Age? Lonely for her teammates who had graduated on time? And to this day, she can't explain what happened that final season, although as March Madness and tournament time neared, she started to turn it around.

But in another one of those cruel twists of fate that seem to plague her, as a repeat of the national championship was in UConn's grasp, she suffered another torn knee ligament, and just like that her college career was over.

That occurred in the Big East tournament championship game against Notre Dame when just minutes before the end of the first half, she fell on her left leg going for an offensive rebound (the first two ACL tears had been to the right knee). Ralph pounded her fist on the floor and writhed in pain while 10,000 people, two teams, and her ashen-faced mother watched in stunned silence.

In the locker room at halftime, her leg once again in that all-too-familiar cumbersome blue leg brace, she told her team she had just tweaked the knee and she'd be back to lead them to another championship. (Senior Svetlana Abrosimova, the other All-American on the team, was already out for the season with a foot injury.) Ralph insisted on coming out for the second half; her appearance set off a raucous standing ovation among the fans, who probably knew she was done. Ralph embraced Abrosimova and spent twenty minutes on her feet cheering for her team. She had left the game as the team's leading scorer (11 points) and also had 6 assists and 3 steals. Notre Dame had led most of the way, but as if the gods were watching over the Huskies, Connecticut won the game when then sophomore guard Sue Bird, who was to go on to light up the women's basketball world herself, took the ball coast to coast for the winning shot at the buzzer. Bird had learned firsthand about the toll that such a devastating injury extracted from a player. Her freshman year, in just her eighth game, she, too, tore her ACL and spent the year rehabbing and watching her teammates from the sidelines. During that season, Bird spoke frequently of how Shea Ralph had been a role model for her in terms of working hard and facing adversity with dignity.

When Ralph went down against Notre Dame, UConn women's basketball trainer Rosemary Ragle was one of the first to her side. Ragle recalls the scene: "She knew what had happened. She kept saying 'I did it again, I did it again,' over and over." Was she in pain? "More devastated than in pain," the trainer recalled.

Ralph insisted on going back out for the second period because the one thing Shea Ralph couldn't tolerate was that "people might see her as a weak individual," the trainer said. "And she didn't want to let her teammates down."

Or her coach.

"Every time I played I wanted to make him proud of me," Ralph said of Auriemma with whom she clashed frequently in epic battles of wills. But through all the highs and lows of Ralph's career, when she shined and when she stunk, he was always watching out for her welfare, making sure to include her in decisions when she couldn't play, encouraging and expressing confidence in her ability to return to the court. In one of the most poignant scenes in UConn women's basketball history, Ralph and Abrosimova, the one hobbling out to the court in a brace, the other on crutches, raised the Big East tournament trophy high over their heads the night of Ralph's injury. Their normally stoic coach, after tugging uncomfortably at his red tie, walked unnoticed across the floor back to the locker room.

After the injury her senior year, Ralph put off the surgery and instead traveled with the team to the NCAA tournament, where they were finally cut down, ironically, by Notre Dame in the national semifinals. (The Irish would go on to win the NCAA championship that year, beating Purdue in the finals two days later after their come-from-behind victory over Connecticut.)

Ragle remembers how quickly Ralph insisted on getting into therapy. She still had every intention of carrying on with a pro career and was in a rush to be ready for the WNBA's May draft. "Her whole attitude toward therapy was 'do it quick, do it right, and get me strong so I can go back out there again,'" Ragle said. Sometimes the zealousness bordered on the dangerous. Several times during the 2001 NCAA tournament, Ragle made sure she was in the fitness center at the hotel when Ralph was there so she wouldn't try to do too much. "She'd always tell me 'Rosie, don't worry. I know you're concerned.'" But then a day or so later, she'd be back to the same aggressive workouts that forced Ragle to keep a watchful eye on her to begin with. "Her whole personality was to work her ass off," the trainer recalled.

Her ACL injury dropped Ralph down to the fortieth player picked in the May 2001 WNBA draft—an indication of how her fortunes had fallen. She knows her stock would have been higher had she gone out her junior year—academically she was a senior with enough credits to graduate—but her reaction to her decision to stay is typical: "I played basketball for my teammates, my family, and my coaches," she said. "The pros are a business, and I knew I'd never find anything like what we had at Connecticut again."

The determination and willpower Ralph displayed through her rehabilitation were qualities that ten or so years earlier squeezed just about all of the life out of Shea Ralph. Since ninth grade, she had suffered from anorexia, brought on, according to her mother, by her desire to look like her Fayetteville cheerleader friends. The fact that most were a foot shorter than Ralph did not inhibit her desire to weigh ninety pounds.

When one day a teammate told her she looked a little chubby, Ralph overreacted and started a crash diet. Slowly, she eliminated food groups as she struggled to keep under 600 calories a day. Some days, her entire food intake consisted of a bowl of dry cereal, a pear, and a plain baked potato. "I was counting the calories in cough drops," she told an audience of college students years later when she had made up her mind that her experiences could help others.

Shea Ralph's Honors at UConn

Sporting News, National Freshman of the Year, 1996–97

USBWA, National Freshman of the Year, 1996–97

Honda Award, women's basketball, 1999–2000

Kodak First-Team All-American, 1999–2000

Kodak Honorable Mention, First Team, All-American, 2000–01

Associated Press, All-America Team: 1998–99, 1999–2000, 2000–01 (the first and last were honorable mention)

USBWA, All-American, 1999–2000

Big East Player of the Year, 1999–2000; Rookie of the Year, 1996–97

She tried to fool people about her illness by wearing bulky sweatshirts and baggy pants, but there were some who couldn't be deceived. "I was always begging her to eat," her mother recalled; soon the matter was out of her hands and into those of physicians and professional counselors. In Ralph's sophomore year, after her high-school basketball team lost in the state championship game, her physician ordered a thorough physical exam after noticing how thin she looked.

His worst fears were confirmed, and he immediately ordered her to gain ten pounds or he would put her in the hospital. At the time she barely weighed one hundred pounds even though she was pushing 6 feet. A few months later, she returned for a checkup, sneaking ankle weights in under her clothes in an attempt to fool the doctor and his scales.

As she grew progressively thinner, there were times she was so weak that her mother had to help her out of bed. Marsha Lake recalls an important basketball game against Fayetteville's biggest rival (both teams were undefeated) in which she watched her daughter sitting doubled over on the bench because her stomach was so cramped up from not eating. That night she scored 30 points—a strange phenomenon shuts down a person's digestive system when they're active—but as soon as the game ended, she was back on the bench hunched over in pain.

All her mother could do was sit and watch her talented daughter self-destruct. "That was the hardest thing to get her through," Marsha Lake recalled years later. "The knees were different. We could fix those. But anorexia—that was up to Shea. I could take her to psychiatrists and nutritionists and cook meals for her, but I was an outsider who was only trying to help."

Shea Ralph in her role as assistant women's basketball coach at Pitt.
Willimantic Chronicle/Jared Ramsdell

Though in some ways the fear of being overweight will always haunt her, in the end her AAU coach's threat to bench her finally made her come to her senses. This was a pivotal point in her career. College coaches were starting to come around, and national high-school honors were at stake. "That ultimatum was the best thing he could have done for me," she said of the coach's order. "I could choose to be skinny or I could choose to play basketball. Basketball was more important."

Ralph is still a fanatic about eating but these days weighs in at a solid 155. In college, because of the muscle from the strenuous conditioning program she set for herself, she tipped the scales at 175 and was hard as a rock.

"We all have our demons that we may never overcome," she says when reflecting on those dark years. These days she's more mature and able to cope. And she also has the young women on her team to think about. "It will always be a part of me," she said of her tendency to skip meals, "but I obviously have it under control. When I get to the point that I can't exercise, I get a little psycho. But if I feel I'm fit, then I don't have problems with eating."

On the rare occasions she allows herself a cupcake or candy, she wakes up feeling like she's gained ten pounds, so the possibility of descent is ever near. And when she feels heavy, "My face swells up, I'm mean to people," her voice trails off, then regains its vigor. "I know 90 percent of it is mental . . . you'd be amazed the power the mind has over the body."

Amazed? Shea Ralph is a living example of the power the mind has over the body—a body that has betrayed her time and time again, whether it was her knees, or her appetite, or most recently, a deformed jaw and crooked teeth, the result of being bashed in the face once too often when she played basketball. For two years, in her mid-twenties, she had to wear braces and her smile was askew. At times she had difficulty talking. She plans to have her jaw realigned and teeth fixed in the future. Her reason: "I want to do something for me. I'm strong enough to know my teeth aren't a reflection of me. But I just want to be able to smile and look pretty in a picture."

"Something for me." No crime in that, nothing to feel guilty about. For most people, that's a top priority. But Shea Ralph was and is a team player. If she knew back in Fayetteville what she knows now, that she'd have her knees operated on five times, that her appearance would be altered, that she would never play competitively after college, would she have taken the same route?

"I'd do it ten times over again. If I had had seven ACLs . . . basketball has shaped who I am," she said. Sure, it's still hard to watch former UConn teammates starring in the pros or playing for their country on the Olympic team. "But I have accepted the terms my life has taken," she said. "And I'm happy with them."

In August 2004 Ralph was asked to speak at a press conference announcing a large grant to Pitt Medical School researchers to study ACL injuries in women. At the time, the Olympics were going on in Athens. When it was Ralph's turn to speak, a rare wave of emotion overcame her. Three of the Olympians (Sue Bird, Diana Taurasi, and Swin Cash) were her Connecticut teammates, she said to a hushed audience. "And that was my dream, too."

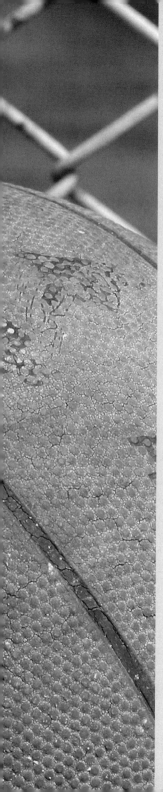

Banner
Years

Visiting teams must be overwhelmed by the sight, whether it's Tennessee with six of its own or a first-round NCAA tournament team, such as lowly Hampton University whom the Huskies beat by seventy-one points on their way to the 2000 national title. There they are: five 10-foot by 20-foot white felt banners, each with the year, national championship, and logo of the Final Four city, attached forever to the Gampel Pavilion's southeast wall some 70 feet above the court.

Each banner tells a different story; some titles were expected, others complete surprises. Two (1995 and 2002) represent undefeated seasons; three (2002–04) represent a three-peat. In all, UConn has been to the Final Four eight times; they came up short in three of them, each time in the semifinals (losing to Virginia in 1991, Tennessee in 1996, and Notre Dame in 2001) but never in the finals. If they get there, they finish the job.

Although the names in the box scores differed from year to year, the winning players all possessed the same quality: a hunger to bring back another championship banner to Storrs, Connecticut, where anything less is often viewed as failure by the fans, the coaching staff, and the team itself. Here are the highlights from each of the eight years UConn reached the Final Four:

1991

This Final Four was in New Orleans, and the site couldn't have been more appropriate for the upset-minded Huskies for whom the 1991 Final Four was a party. No one expected them to get this far, even though Connecticut had put together the best season in team history, going 29–5, including victories over Auburn (a perennial SEC contender), Big 12 power Iowa State, and a Big East tournament championship. It almost came to a grinding halt in the second round of the NCAA East region, when Connecticut nearly lost to twelfth-seed Toledo, but Kerry Bascom had 39 points, including the winning three-point play. The game gave them momentum: Their next stop was the Palestra, in coach Geno Auriemma's hometown of Philadelphia, where they knocked off a pair of Atlantic Coast Conference teams (NC State and Clemson) to advance to their first-ever Final Four at the sold-out Lakefront Arena, which held 7,903. There they ran into an ACC opponent they couldn't get past, falling 61–55 to Virginia, Auriemma's former team.

"We were so excited to be there—in retrospect, too much," recalled Meghan Pattyson-Cuomo, one of a trio of players from Pennsylvania whom Auriemma had brought in three years earlier to give Bascom a surrounding cast. Being followed around by Robin Roberts and the ESPN-TV crew, dining on expensive Cajun meals, having a police escort to and from a first-class hotel, dancing at parties on Bourbon Street—these are the memories the players took home with them as well as the haunting recollection of a game they might have won had Bascom not gotten into early foul trouble and only managed 14 points. "That team was special," said associate head coach Chris Dailey. "We didn't start anyone over 6'2", we had one All-American, but we passed well and played good defense." Virginia forward Tonya Cardoza remembers trying to guard Bascom, who wore her down so badly she was only 6 of 14. "I remember taking Connecticut a little lightly," she said. She found out three years later that she could never take UConn lightly, after joining Auriemma as an assistant and returning to the Final Four seven times since.

1995

A three-year drought was to pass before the next Final Four, but when it came, it rushed in and took the women's basketball world by storm. Connecticut got back on track in 1994, when they made it to the Final Eight in the NCAA East region. But the Tar

Heels of North Carolina beat them handily and then validated their worth by winning the 1994 national championship.

Revenge was on the minds of the Huskies as the 1994–95 season began, especially for senior Rebecca Lobo, the 1990–91 national high-school player of the year, who passed up more prominent basketball (and academic) schools such as Stanford because she wanted to make a difference in a program. The nonconference schedule was fairly soft leading into the season, with the exception of the January 16 game at Gampel Pavilion, a game circled on everybody's calendar. The Huskies, ranked second in the country at the time, were playing Tennessee, which marched into the arena loaded with high-school and college All-Americans as the number one team in the country. Some thirty-five minutes of basketball later, with Lobo on the bench with five fouls, UConn's 6'7" junior center Kara Wolters scored on a layup and 5'6" junior point guard Jen Rizzotti sank a three to give UConn a 69–57 lead. As the clock ticked down (the final score was 77–66), Lobo exploded off the bench with a single finger thrust in the air. "I'll never forget this as long as I live," she was to say later.

But other memories were to be stronger: The Huskies held on to the number one ranking through the season and entered the NCAA tournament as the top seed, having gone 29–0 to that point and anticipating a rematch with the mighty Lady Vols in the championship game at the Target Center in Minneapolis. Looking back, Rizzotti called the Tennessee win in Storrs a "coming-out party. The year before we had beaten Auburn and Virginia . . . such big names in women's basketball, but this was a team that had been to the NCAAs every year," she said. Rizzotti remembers feeling Connecticut was on the verge of something special a year earlier when she was a sophomore, but "we didn't get respect until we beat Tennessee. We had finally arrived. We finally got the game that put us on the map." Lobo recalled, "We were all wide-eyed. Could this really be happening? None of us ever thought we were going to be undefeated."

The team felt good about itself going into the postseason. "We were really confident, but at the same time we felt like the underdog," Rizzotti said. To keep things on an even keel, Auriemma played up that role. "He never let us believe we got respect from the outside," she recalled. "He always made us feel we had to prove ourselves to the outside world." Connecticut almost didn't make it to Minneapolis, barely escaping with a 4-point win over their old nemesis Virginia in the East regional second round at Gampel Pavilion. As the first half wound down, the Cavaliers went on a 34–8 run to lead by 7 points at the break. It was to be the first time the Huskies trailed at the half in any game that season. But UConn came out flying to start the second period and went on a 12–5 run to grab back the lead, which they held onto for a trip to the Final Four. Wolters's 18 points, Lobo's 6 blocked shots, and Nykesha Sale's 4 steals made it possible.

The national semifinal against Stanford, with a trio of front court trees, turned into a joke as Connecticut rolled to an 87–60 win and the final showdown against Tennessee, a game that both teams had anticipated since the close of day January 16. "We had approached the Stanford game with a ton of confidence, but Tennessee was different," said Rizzotti. "It's easier to play with the frame of mind that everyone expects you to win." Tennessee, which has always had trouble scoring points, was held to 36 percent shooting from the floor, while the Huskies shot nearly 50 percent. It was the difference that made a difference.

And when it was over, once again Lobo was to race across a basketball court with her finger raised in the air. With 34 points, 17 rebounds, and 4 blocks in two games, she was named tournament MVP. "We had been swept up in something that was bigger than all of us," she recalled years later.

1996

With the graduation of Lobo and starting guard Pam Webber, the Huskies once again had to fight for respect. But they had weapons: Nykesha Sales, who would go on to be a two-time All-American, was now a sophomore and starter; Rizzotti was a year older, as was senior Jamelle Elliott, a tough 6' forward who played bigger than she was in both height and heart. But the regular season schedule was much tougher—Connecticut was starting to be recognized as a national force—and the Huskies struggled against the tougher teams, including Louisiana Tech and Georgia (the latter handing them a rare Gampel defeat). The highlight of the season was a 59–53 win at Tennessee's Thompson-Boling Arena (before 24,000) ending the Lady Vols' record-setting sixty-nine-game home winning streak.

After that, everything pointed to a national championship rematch between the two rivals. Connecticut breezed through the first four rounds of the NCAA tournament, then defeated Southeast Conference (SEC) power Vanderbilt by 10 points in the national semifinal. However, the South was to rise again in a nail-biting national final against Tennessee (who else?) at the Charlotte Coliseum in North Carolina. During regulation, the lead changed hands a dozen times, but just when it looked like it

Nykesha Sales is UConn's all-time scoring leader at 2,178 points.
University of Connecticut Division of Athletics

was going to stay in SEC hands for good, Sales (28 points in forty-two minutes) hit a three-point jumper with 4 seconds left to send it into overtime. By this time, Wolters and Elliott had fouled out, leaving Connecticut vulnerable in the post and at the foul line. Tennessee was 4 for 4 in the final seconds to take the trophy back to Knoxville with an 88–83 victory over their archrival. The national championship title was to be the first of three successive titles for the Lady Vols, making Tennessee and Connecticut (2002–04) the only two teams in women's basketball history to achieve such a feat.

Looking back on the 1996 experience, Rizzotti said the team was just relieved to get to the Final Four. "There was so much talk of not being that good with Rebecca graduating, I remember Jamelle and I feeling we had to get back," said Rizzotti. "There was such intense pressure that we didn't even enjoy the regular season. . . . We just had to get back to the Final Four because no one thought we were going to. Getting there was a huge weight off our shoulders."

2000

Powered by the two best players in the game, Shea Ralph and Svetlana Abrosimova, an All-America backcourt of ball hogs, aggressive leaders, and fierce scoring rivals, all signs pointed to Connecticut's second national championship. And after a three-year drought without a title, dreams came true once again. Abrosimova, particularly, was unique: At seventeen, she came to the United States from her native St. Petersburg, Russia, barely able to speak English. Auriemma had been tipped off to her skills by an American high-school coach with Russian connections. For four years, coach and player were at each others' throats: both equally stubborn, both equally driven to achieve. The triumvirate of clashing egos was completed by Ralph, who had twisted and molded the team in her image.

A deathless competitor from North Carolina, Ralph had willed herself into greatness, despite two bad knees and an average amount of natural athletic talent. For Ralph, everything was an awkward struggle. But where she moved around the court like a gangly puppy, Abrosimova was a seamless greyhound of a player, waltzing her way coast to coast to pull up on a dime and score. The two were surrounded by a bevy of talent: Sue Bird, the point guard who had grown into the job after sitting out her freshman year with a torn ACL; sleek, athletic Swin Cash, who had been a starter since her first year; tall, elegant Kelly Schumacher, who simmered on the back burner for three years before finally coming into her own; and the enforcers—juniors Asjha Jones, quiet and studious, and Tamika Williams, loquacious, brash, and overly sensitive to injury, but a demon under the boards when she came off the bench.

"It was like a fairy-tale story . . . we were ranked number one and supposed to win," recalled Williams, now an assistant coach at Ohio State. "It was a pivotal year. We had lost Sue Bird the first year, so we were doing what we were supposed to do our freshman year," she said. The 1999–2000 version of the Huskies was probably the greatest team they were ever to field, but a loss to Tennessee at Gampel (their only loss in a 37–1 season) slightly taints that judgment.

For Auriemma the Final Four was particularly stressful since it was at the First Union Center in his hometown of Philadel-

Members of the 2000 team, from left: Tamika Williams, Svetlana Abrosimova (in front), Asjha Jones, and Shea Ralph. University of Connecticut Division of Athletics

phia. The area papers were full of "return of the conquering hero" stories, and even rival steak-and-cheese submarine sandwich shops (the biggest two improbably named Geno's and Pat's) got into the competition. In the end Geno's subs (and his starters) prevailed, sending Tennessee packing in an easy 71–52 victory. Shea Ralph, Final Four MVP, was the high scorer for UConn with 15 points; her personal nemesis, Svetlana Abrosimova, in close pursuit with 14. Schumacher also rose to the occasion with 9 blocks, still an NCAA title game record.

Having been knocked out in the Sweet Sixteen a year earlier, the team was driven to not let the same thing happen again. "Once we got to the Final Four, there was no way we were losing," Bird said. Shootaround for the title game was calm, a sign of what was to come. The Lady Vols went to their strength and dominated the boards during the title game, but once again the Husky defense did the job, holding their rivals to only 16 of 51 from the floor.

After the victory, the players carried their coach off the floor. Auriemma, his wavy hair barely visible over the heads of his players, lay in a crumpled heap as the spectacle unfolded. After the celebrating died down, Williams and Bird quietly visited the coach in his hotel room. "There he was puffing on a cigar, just chillin'," Williams recalled.

2001

With everyone returning, there was every expectation that the national championship would stay in Storrs another season. In addition, the team had the added services of a talented freshman from California named Diana Taurasi, who was to prove her worth as first off the bench from the first game of the season.

Once again UConn split with Tennessee during the regular season, but a loss at Notre Dame in early January may have foretold what was in store. As the season wore on, injury and bum luck caught up with the Huskies. In early February Abrosimova, now a senior, suffered a stress fracture during a loss in Knoxville that immediately ended her collegiate career. On senior night her parents, out of Russia for the first time in their lives, flanked their daughter as she hobbled out to the center of the court to say farewell to the fans. But despite her injury, the prospects for back-to-back national championships remained bright. After all, they still had Bird, Jones, Williams, Taurasi, and the indomitable Shea Ralph, who had struggled during the regular season. Surely she would wake up in the postseason—which she did, but so did her bad knee. In a first-round NCAA game against Long Island she tore her ACL yet another time and ended her college career on her back under the home-team basket.

Although the junior class (whose rallying cry became "do it for Shea and Svet") may have been individually better athletes, without the senior leadership they weren't ready to defend their title. Notre Dame, whom the Huskies had beaten at the buzzer a month earlier for the Big East tournament championship, had the last laugh in the national semifinals in St. Louis. Although they had a 12-point lead at the half, the Huskies couldn't hang on and ended up losing by 15 points to send the Irish to their first national title. "By the time all was said and done, we had lost two games in the regular season and our two All-Americans," Bird said. The freshman Taurasi, who had been outstanding her first year, got a quick lesson in college basketball at the highest level, shooting an uncharacteristic 1 of 15 from the field against the Irish. The picture of her coach kneeling in front of her as she sat on the bench, her head in her hands, will be locked forever in the memories of Connecticut fans. The loss, he told her, was a team responsibility, not her own.

"That game still goes down as one of my worst defeats ever," said Bird. "I'll never forget it."

2002

There are some, including their head coach, who think this was the greatest women's basketball team ever put together. So when the four seniors—Bird, Jones, Williams, and Cash—assembled that warm mid-October day for their first practice ever as starters together (Taurasi was the fifth starter), the expectations for success were higher than in the history of the program. No one disappointed.

"From the start we talked about getting back what should have been ours the year before," Bird recalled. "Coach charged this senior class because he felt it was us who didn't step up in the 2001 Final Four . . . that we had a chance and we choked. There was no way any of us was going to let that happen again."

The team was 33–0 going into the NCAA tournament that year, having easily dispatched North Carolina, Vanderbilt, Louisiana Tech, Oklahoma, Tennessee, and the entire Big East during the regular season. In doing so they led the nation in seven of sixteen offensive and defensive statistical categories. This year the NCAA tournament committee structured the brackets so that they would meet the Lady Vols in the national

Who Are the Top Dogs?

What was the greatest UConn team ever? Many would say the answer is a toss-up between the two UConn women's squads that went undefeated, although the 2000 team, which went 37–1, losing at home against Tennessee on its way to a national championship, is hard to leave out. But back to the undefeateds. In 1995 the Huskies were 35–0 and captured their first NCAA championship. Not everyone believed they were the best, until they started putting away opponents one by one, picking them off like picking off errant passes and driving for a layup. They were aided immeasurably by a freshman from Bloomsbury, Connecticut, in Nykesha Sales (the best player from the state to ever play the game), first off the bench (11.4 points and more than 2 steals per game) and the women's basketball team's eventual leading scorer of all time (2,178 points).

In 2002 the team went 39–0, but this was a different situation since with four All-Americans, they were expected to win it all and they did. Confidence, the experience and harmony of playing together for four years (four of the five were seniors) plus a dynamite sophomore named Taurasi made them unbeatable. Like seasoned professionals, they went through the year with calmness, confidence, and courage—biding their time until the NCAA tournament, when they beat six opponents by an average of 27 points a game. That season the Huskies never trailed in the second half in any of its thirty-nine games, and more astounding, in a total of 1,560 minutes played that season, they only trailed 49 minutes and 59 seconds and that by no more than 6 points.

Of the individuals, Rebecca Lobo (1995), Jen Rizzotti (1996), Kara Wolters (1997), and Sue Bird (2002) were all named national players of the year by a number of different organizations and awards committees. Here are the season statistics for the starting lineups of those two over-the-top teams:

1995

Rebecca Lobo: 17.1 points a game, 9.8 rebounds a game

Jennifer Rizzotti: 12.5 points a game, 4.6 assists a game

Kara Wolters: 15.2 points a game, 6.2 rebounds a game

Jamelle Elliott: 10.9 points a game, 8.1 rebounds a game

Pam Webber: 4.6 points a game, 4.1 assists per game

2002

Swin Cash: 14.9 points a game, 8.6 rebounds per game

Sue Bird: 14.4 points a game, 5.9 assists a game

Tamika Williams: 10.1 points a game, 6.9 rebounds a game

Asjha Jones: 14.0 points a game, 6.6 rebounds a game

Diana Taurasi: 14.6 points a game, 5.3 assists per game

semifinal rather than the title game. The Lady Vols were no match. Connecticut held them to just 31.4 percent shooting from the floor while shooting 44.6 percent themselves, and the Huskies cruised into the national final against the second seed, Oklahoma Sooners, having beaten their biggest rivals two days earlier by 23 points.

In the final Connecticut put on an offensive show in the Alamo. The four seniors combined for 65 of the 82 points, and Taurasi added 13 even though the Huskies' 21 turnovers were a national championship game record. But the Huskies were runners, a style of play that leads to quick turnovers. As long as the points were coming, it didn't matter.

Although Connecticut let Oklahoma close the gap during the game, it didn't matter either. This was a team of destiny, a well-

2002: The Stats Don't Lie

Here are the final scoring and rebounding averages and block and assist totals for the starting five of the 39–0 team of 2002:

	Points	Rebounds	Blocks/Assists/Steals
Swin Cash	14.9	8.6	55 blocks, 55 steals
Diana Taurasi	14.5	4.1	208 assists; 46 blocks
Sue Bird	14.4	3.4	231 assists, 96 steals
Asjha Jones	14.0	6.6	61 blocks
Tamika Williams	10.1	6.9	52 steals

Swin Cash (left) and Sue Bird (right) celebrate a national championship in 2002 with President Bush at the White House. University of Connecticut Division of Athletics

oiled machine comprised of confident, skilled young women who felt their fate was totally in their control. "No matter how close it got, we were not going to lose. You could just feel it. . . . there was never any worry," Bird said. In many ways they approached games as a surgeon does surgery: They came into an arena, scrubbed up, made the cuts, performed the operation, dusted off their hands, and left as winners. They did this thirty-nine times and never lost. Two months later the four seniors were among the top six players selected in the WNBA draft.

"Jamelle [Elliott] used to tell us that we had never really won a national championship until we went undefeated," Williams recalled of the ribbing they took from their assistant coach, a member of the 35–0 team of 1995. "She always used to rub that in our face. But that night we ran to her and rubbed it in her face."

2003

This was the year the Huskies were not supposed to win a national title. After all, two All-Americans were gone, and other than Diana Taurasi, none of those remaining had played more than fifteen minutes in the previous Final Fours. It was a team with a heavy burden on its back, but it was also a team that fed off the "they can't repeat" attitude of the analysts. (Preseason rankings had them as low as twelfth; most had Duke winning it all.) But, as it turned out, it was a team that did repeat—a team that Auriemma, not easy with the compliments, was to say later he was the most proud of in his coaching history.

The personnel: point guard Maria Conlon, a sharpshooter at Connecticut's Seymour High School, she had been used as a backup to Sue Bird and then only to rest the starter in blowouts. But Conlon was smart and had learned, both by watching and going up against Bird in practice. Everything was in place; she only had to execute. Behind her were Jessica Moore and Ashley Battle, technically juniors, but since both had redshirted their freshman year, they were really only in their first full year of basketball. Each had put together a pretty good season: Moore, who had sat out her first year because the coaching staff didn't think she was ready for Division I play, proved that she was ready for prime time and started all thirty-eight games at center. Averaging 5.9 rebounds a contest (second only to Taurasi), Moore was quick and athletic for a 6'3" center. Her weakness was her passivity around the basket. Instead of demanding the shot, she waited until someone noticed her and ended up scoring only 5.4 points a game. Battle, who sat out her freshman year with elbow problems, was the first off the bench; her defense was her strong suit (she had 55 steals in an average twenty-two minutes in thirty-seven games) and had been named Big East Defensive Player of the Year for her tenacity in forcing turnovers. But she wasn't much of a scorer, and at 6' it was hard to find a spot for her in the lineup: Too small for a forward, but not a good enough ball handler for the backcourt, she had carved her niche by stopping the other team's toughest player. The other major players were a trio of highly promising freshmen: Barbara Turner, a strong, bull-headed 6' forward who played like she was 6'5"; Ann Strother, a highly sought-after 6'2" guard, who showed flashes of quickness and shooting accuracy but whose tough-mindedness was often in question; and 6'2" forward Willnett Crockett, clearly the strongest player on the team, but given to letting minor injuries affect her play. And then there was Taurasi: jumpy, cocky, but determined to continue the winning tradition and willing and able to take the team on her back.

The road to the Final Four was treacherous, with games against Big East rival Boston College in the East Regional Sweet Sixteen (a team whose familiarity could cut both ways, players said: Each knew the other's strengths and weaknesses) and number-two-seed, Purdue (UConn was the top seed), which got an early taste of the Huskies' defensive pressure in the Final Eight by missing 13 straight shots. At the half, the defending champs led by 19 points, but in the second period, the Boilermakers boiled over and outscored UConn 42–32, though still not enough to overcome their first-half deficit. UConn moved on to the Georgia Dome for their fourth straight Final Four; Purdue went home wondering what could have been.

The national semifinal was against a taller, equally tough Texas team coached by Jody Conradt, one of the most successful in the game. On paper it appeared as if the Longhorns would roll over Connecticut. But they lacked one element: Diana Taurasi. She scored 26 points in thirty-eight minutes and helped her team overcome a 9-point deficit late in the game with a three-pointer and a pair of steals. By comparison, the 73–68 NCAA championship victory over Tennessee was a walk in the park. Taurasi, who plays her best against the Lady Vols (Coach Pat Summitt once said her happiest moment would be when that girl graduated), lit them up with 28 points and the second straight national championship was in the bank. The 2003 Final Four will be remembered as a rite of passage for the less experienced players. In the semifinal, Crockett had the game of her life, holding her ground against the taller, stronger Longhorns for 10 rebounds; in the title game, Conlon played thirty-nine flawless minutes without a turnover, and Strother and Turner combined for 27 points.

Later, Auriemma had to acknowledge that the team was better than he had anticipated. Or at least more motivated and sick of hearing that they were too young and inexperienced to win another championship. They finished the season an astounding 37–1, their only loss to Villanova in the Big East championship game. (Villanova was to have a banner year itself, making it to the NCAA Final Eight before losing to Tennessee.) After they won the national championship, some UConn players said that until they defeated Tennessee in the regular season (Taurasi led the team in a come-from-behind overtime win), it didn't feel real. The loss to Villanova was a brief detour, but once past that, "the next six games we played our best basketball," Conlon recalled.

2004

If the 2003 season taught them that they could win against all odds, the following year was to teach them they could lose against all odds. With everyone back from the 2003 championship year, it was only natural that they would be ranked number one in the early weeks. Taurasi was in her final year; Turner, Strother, and Crockett were a year older; and Moore and Battle had passed the test of playing at the highest levels. The freshmen 6'5" Liz Sherwood, an AAU teammate of Strother's in Colorado, and Kiana Robinson, a swift little guard who was being groomed for the future (both transferred at the end of the season), couldn't add much but were bodies to spell relief for the major players. As it turned out, the season teetered on the brink of disaster from early January until the very end. First there was the problem with Taurasi, who constantly struggled with nagging back, ankle, and various other injuries. She was frustrated because the team didn't gel, and although she was still willing to carry them to their third consecutive NCAA national championship, it became increasingly clear that she couldn't do it alone.

"Last year was the hardest in my twenty-three years of basketball," then senior Morgan Valley was to comment when the season was well behind her. She and Conlon spoke of how brutal Auriemma made the practices, of bad karma with some of the younger players, of slumps by the sophomores. But more significantly, the team struggled in big games. The much-awaited January 3 confrontation with Duke at the Hartford Civic Center became emblematic of the problems. The Huskies outplayed the Blue Devils for thirty-seven minutes but then uncharacteristically lost their composure when Duke went into a full court press and forced 7 turnovers that led to 10 points and a tie with 40 seconds left. Taurasi got the lead back again on a jumper with 5 seconds left, but then Duke guard Lindsey Harding drove the length of the court and at the last second flipped the ball to long-range specialist Jessica Foley on the right side. The Australian off the bench drained a three as the buzzer sounded.

The stunned silence that greeted the Huskies as they stood dazed on the court (while the Blue Devils celebrated in a pile-up on the floor) was to work its way into the locker room and onto the practice floor for several weeks after that. "Practice was like being in a mortuary," recalled Conlon. "After Duke, we felt like the worst team in the country."

Connecticut won its next two games against weaker Big East opponents, but then on January 13, now ranked fourth, found themselves once again in unfriendly territory, as they traveled to South Bend to play Notre Dame. The unranked Irish had been struggling all season; a win over UConn was just what they needed to get them set for the grueling campaign ahead. And it was just what they got. Unlike the Duke game, UConn trailed most of the time, but with 5 seconds remaining, Taurasi got them within 2 points. That was as close as they came. Once again, in the clutch they were helpless, missing six straight shots and losing the ball twice in turnovers to walk off the court (where pandemonium had ensued) defeated, 66–51.

A close shave with Boston College four days later didn't do much to get the team (or the entire state, for that matter) out of its funk, but then as luck would have it, there was still the Tennessee game to recoup some losses. And in Knoxville, too. With everyone chipping in—four players were in double figures—and the defense once again leading the way (they held the Lady Vols to 39 percent shooting), Connecticut came back to Storrs with an 81–67 victory and a new lease on life. "We pulled it together in Tennessee," recalled Conlon.

The Huskies cruised through the rest of the Big East schedule until once again, Villanova's slow, deliberate style of play tripped them up and they lost their third game of the year. The Big East tournament, held in Hartford for the first time, was the start of postseason play, but again they tripped: Boston College, always a solid, offensive squad, shot an unreal 63 percent from the floor in the tournament semifinal and sent UConn packing in their own backyard. It was the second straight year they had been eliminated from the Big East tournament. "It's easier to win the national championship than the Big East tournament," Auriemma was to comment later. Connecticut would redeem itself in front of a Civic Center crowd nearly three weeks later, defeating a tough UC–Santa Barbara team in the NCAA Sweet Sixteen before knocking off Penn State, seeded first in the region (UConn was second) two nights later in the Final

Eight. That victory lifted them to their fifth straight Final Four, where they held off Minnesota and All-America point guard Lindsay Whalen in the national semifinals. (Whalen, coming back from a wrist injury, was to become a favorite of Connecticut fans that following summer as the first-round draft pick of the WNBA's Connecticut Sun.) UConn was again led by Taurasi (18 points) and a big three-pointer by junior Ann Strother, who next to Taurasi was the team's best shooter. This gave UConn an 11-point victory, even though the game played a lot closer.

Tennessee (who else?) stood between them and a three-peat as national champions. "We've had a lot of ups and downs and we've handled them well," Taurasi said on the eve of the April 6 title game. The Lady Vols had come into the final game through the back door, pulling out 2-point wins in the final seconds of the three games leading up to it. A team of destiny? Perhaps, but Coach Pat Summitt was more comfortable with the phrase "living on the edge."

As it turned out, Connecticut was the team of destiny in 2004, defeating Tennessee 70–61 in the national final. At one point the Huskies enjoyed a 16-point lead but mistakenly let the Lady Vols back in, and they cut the lead to 4. But that was as close as they would come. After last-minute losses to Duke and Notre Dame, the Huskies had finally learned how to hold on. Taurasi's 17 points led the way, and she was named MVP of the Final Four for the second straight year.

Players were to say later that the 2003–04 season taught them how to lose. But it also taught them they could still win. The team, which went 31–4, had come full circle in 2004, returning to New Orleans for Connecticut's eighth Final Four in fourteen years. This time, the games were held at the New Orleans Arena before 18,211 fans, nearly three times as many as had witnessed the Huskies' first trip to that city thirteen years earlier. The increase in fans showed how much the game had grown in little more than a decade. And a key element in that growth was the University of Connecticut women's basketball team, an ever-changing group of young, talented women for whom there was and will continue to be one constant: hanging yet another national championship banner on the Gampel Pavilion wall.

Mothers and Daughters

Three of the best players to ever wear UConn women's basketball uniforms found out in painful ways that athletics can help them through the toughest times, even when it came to the life and death of their mothers.

The three—Leigh Curl (1981–85), arguably the most successful professionally of any other player; Rebecca Lobo (1991–95), whose brains and skills made UConn a national name; and Kara Wolters (1992–96), whose 6'7" height may have changed how big girls think of themselves—have had personal tragedies in their lives that put in perspective the wins and losses of their athletic careers. Curl lost her mother when she was just fourteen, and Wolters at twenty-seven, a few years following an All-America career at UConn. Of the three, Lobo was the only fortunate one. Though her mother RuthAnn Lobo, had a life-threatening bout with breast cancer, she emerged alive and healthy, a miracle patient as far as her doctors and her family are concerned. Throughout their lives, the players have drawn upon their mothers' support of their athletic pursuits. And their mothers, despite hardships they may have been undergoing, remained loyal and supportive to their daughters, always taking pride in their accomplishments.

Leigh Curl was a gangly kid (she would grow to close to 6'2"), a tomboy, really, growing up as the second eldest of five girls and a boy in Pittsburgh. On Christmas morning, it was hard to tell her pile of presents under the tree from those of her brother: baseballs, gloves, bats, hockey sticks, team jerseys, tickets to Penguins and Pirates games—they stuck out from among the pile reflecting the girl's devotion to and success at just about every sport she played. Behind all of this was her mother, Barbara Curl, a Pittsburgh housewife and three-letter athlete at a Catholic high school for girls in the city before marrying Frank Curl at nineteen. Leigh's dad put the basketball hoop up in the front yard, but it was her mom who was outside shooting with the kids, playing softball at picnics, and carting her kids to their games. The achievements of Curl, now a highly successful orthopedic surgeon and professor at Johns Hopkins Medical School in Baltimore as well as the chief orthopedic surgeon for the Baltimore

Ravens football team, reflect her honors-level scholastic record at UConn and beyond as well as her focus and determination. "Both of my parents supported my interest in sports in an era when being a tomboy was not necessarily cool or the societal norm as it is today," Curl said referring to what it was like growing up in the pre-politically correct years of the 1960s and 1970s. Her mom's only issue was that her daughter, at the time a gifted high-school softball player, not wear her cap to the dinner table.

One Monday morning as Leigh got ready for school (she was in ninth grade at the time), Curl noticed her mother lying on the sofa, instead of helping to get the children ready for the day. When she returned home from school that day, her father told his children that their mother was "bleeding in the brain and was very sick." By Wednesday when she came home from school, Curl had a "weird sense that something was amiss." Extra cars were parked out front and when she finally entered the house, after hunkering down in the woods for a while, she could see her dad had been crying. One of her grandparents informed her "Mommy died." "All of a sudden the whole world was turning on its heels," she said. For the next few days, they mourned, on Sunday they buried thirty-four-year-old Barbara Curl, who had succumbed to a brain aneurysm November 2, 1977, and Monday the kids were back on the school bus as if nothing had happened. Her grief-stricken father refused to allow the kids to speak of her mother or her death. The natural grieving process, it would appear, had to be deferred or ignored altogether. "I had to suppress all this emotion," Curl recalled.

Not long after her mother died, Curl's father remarried and home life became tumultuous. "It was not a place I wanted to be," she said. So she dove into academics and athletics, spending every moment studying or hanging out with teammates at their homes on weekends. "My friends and my teammates became my family," she said. This was a particularly difficult transition for Curl, who had been such a homebody while her mother was alive that a visit to her grandparents was often traumatic. When it came time for college, the University of Connecticut made her an offer she couldn't refuse, so she left home to study and play basketball in Storrs. "I really don't think I would have gone that far from home had my mother not died," Curl said of her decision to attend Connecticut. "Her death made me more independent. It forced me to find myself a little."

Curl became the best player on losing teams (she scored 1,388 career points and is among the top ten players of all time in rebounds) but in the classroom she was a winner. Accepted to the prestigious University Scholars Program, Curl was a dean's list student in biology and to this day the best student her honors advisor, biology professor Ted Taigen, has ever had. "She was gifted physically and intellectually," he said, "always coming up with great ideas and with the endurance to follow through despite a grueling schedule." It was Taigen who insisted she apply to Johns Hopkins Medical School (Curl was thinking of Pitt because it was closer to home). She was admitted to Hopkins and has distinguished herself ever since in her specialty of orthopedic surgery. Her education in the classroom and in labs was supplemented by important lessons she learned through athletics. At the same time, the disappointment of being on a bad team year after year was mitigated by the classroom. "Basketball was a means to an end," she said. "And in the end, the pain of losing goes away with age. I had other things going for me. I was bitter for a while, but that went away."

Leigh Curl (right) during her playing days at UConn in the early 1980s.
University of Connecticut Division of Athletics

Physician, Heal Thyself

Dr. Leigh Curl has accumulated a number of academic and professional achievement awards throughout her life. In 1998, with her former undergraduate advisor Professor Ted Taigen at her side, she was inducted into the GTE/CoSIDA Academic All-America Hall of Fame, only the sixth woman to achieve such a distinction. It is the highest academic honor there is for a former collegiate athlete.

Her other academic awards earned during her playing career at UConn (1981–85) included two-time Academic All-American, valedictorian of her 1985 graduating class, summa cum laude in biology, and 1985 Big East Women's Basketball Scholar-Athlete. On the court, she scored 1,388 points and is currently sixteenth in career scoring at UConn. She was a four-year starter and captain of the team for two years.

But because she was not permitted to mourn her mother at the time, closure following her death was still elusive. That pain was finally revisited decades later when Curl, herself, turned thirty-four, and she realized she was the same age her mother was when she died. Her father still doesn't talk about it—she suspects the pain was too great for him—but it's no longer a taboo subject among the rest of the family. Three nieces bear the middle name Barbara, and pictures of their mother are in every child's home. But the marker on her grave has no mention of her six children, and Curl doesn't go very often because she said she finds the cemetery "very cold and lifeless, which is not how I remember her, so I don't find much comfort there." Ten years ago, another traumatic event befell someone close to Curl, and this helped her come to terms—at last—with her mother's death. She has done the best she can, it's her nature, but there will always remain that hole in the continuity of her life, that point in time, when she had to let go of her mother's life and the memory of that life, all too quickly and abruptly.

■ ■ ■

In some ways the children of RuthAnn Lobo also were in denial—only their issues centered around their mother's breast cancer, which was diagnosed in December 1993. At the time, RuthAnn's youngest daughter, Rebecca, was a junior and the star player on the UConn women's basketball team.

One unforgettable night, RuthAnn's children, two daughters and a son, came to terms with their future. It was warm that May evening when the trio of young adults left their home in South-wick, Massachusetts, for Hartford where they planned to have a few beers and, they hoped, some old fashioned sibling fun. It had

RuthAnn (left) and Rebecca Lobo announcing a scholarship fund.
University of Connecticut Division of Athletics

been a while. All three were in college, and since their mother's diagnosis and treatment five months earlier, things had been tense.

Maybe it was the beer. Maybe it was the release from the day-to-day stress. Maybe it was being away from their parents. Maybe it was time. As they were driving home, one of them suddenly blurted out the heretofore unspoken question: "Are you afraid mom's going to die?" The question might have hung in the air for a minute or two. But it wasn't long before the floodgates opened, and all three were talking at once, expressing their anxiety, their fears, their hopes. "Because we had all felt guilty thinking 'what if mom died,' we had never talked about it," recalled Lobo; everyone was too scared to mention the unmentionable and so the three of them bore their burdens in the private silence of their own hearts and minds. But that night something magical happened, and each of them spoke freely about the possibility that their lives could change forever. "That night it was a huge weight off our shoulders," Lobo said.

Rebecca Lobo's parents are tall, dignified people (father 6'5", mother 5'11", siblings over 6 feet) who made sure their children grew up with Christian values and pride in themselves. Even if occasionally a cruel classmate called Lobo, who is 6'4", the Jolly Green Giant, it didn't bother her because she liked being tall. In fact, she remembers thinking at school dances, when the boys came up to her waist, "When are they going to grow up?" Basketball, her passion from an early age, had a lot to do with her acceptance of her height. "I loved the game so much, I knew my height was an advantage," she said. "Sometimes I got frustrated when I was buying clothes, not because I was too tall but because I thought the manufacturers didn't make them long enough."

This love and devotion to the sport (as well as her studies— Lobo, like Curl, was an honors student in college) kept both her and her mother going during the latter's weeks and months of surgery, chemotherapy, and radiology. The absence of self-pity on both their parts characterized their resolve during this traumatic period. That tone was set from the moment RuthAnn Lobo told her daughter that she had breast cancer in the stands of Gampel Pavilion after a game against Virginia on December 11, 1993. "I waited until after the game because I didn't want to impact the play," she said. (UConn won the game; Lobo was the leading scorer.) "Then we sat down in Gampel, and I told her I had some news . . . that I had discovered a lump and it was, in fact, cancer. That it had popped up out of nowhere." Connecticut associate head coach Chris Dailey was there at RuthAnn's invitation to give the girl support, and naturally, as she wept, it was necessary. Her mother was undeterred. "I was very matter of fact about it: I told her 'You do what you have to do and I'll do what I have to do.' " And then to lighten things up she added: "Your father isn't a breast man, anyhow."

Lobo listened to her mother carefully and took her advice, continuing with her schoolwork and her work on the court. "I never thought of leaving school. Basketball was the only time I didn't think about her. Coach Auriemma yelling at me was the best therapy," she said.

The Wednesday before Christmas, RuthAnn Lobo had a lumpectomy of the right breast and within a few days learned twenty-eight of her thirty-three lymph nodes had to be taken as well. The basketball team was on a break, so Rebecca was home for the recuperation—as brief as it was—and the family put it on its best face to celebrate Christmas. "I remember looking at the tree and wondering if it was my last Christmas," RuthAnn said. "It was an emotional Christmas," recalled Rebecca. "She didn't know if she would live to see another one."

What followed was a difficult period of chemotherapy. "I remember the first time I saw my mother with a wig," Rebecca said. "We were stretching before a game and she was in the stands. The sight brought tears to my eyes. I was seeing someone who looked so different." But for RuthAnn, not much changed. She planned her chemotherapy treatments so that she would never miss a basketball game (home and within driving distance); in fact, they became something to look forward to. And she only missed a week of work as a guidance counselor at Granby Memorial Middle School in Granby, Connecticut. As word got out about her condition, prayer groups formed throughout the state.

These days, she's a healthy, active, robust woman who has been cancer-free for more than a decade. Her doctor calls her his miracle patient. "One of the most significant pieces of my recovery was my trust in God," RuthAnn Lobo said. "I wasn't saying 'OK, God, take over,' but I had read a lot of books on God's desire to heal. The thing that was hard was that I had expected to call the shots, but God did, not me," she says.

"My mother has inner strength," Rebecca said. "Her faith made her stronger." Rebecca said her family never saw their mother as a sick person, but as someone battling something, much like an athlete battles the other team. "All of us talk of her as cured, even though she's said to be still in remission," said Rebecca. "The doctors won't use the word *cured*, but we have since the moment she had her hair back."

As might be expected, the Lobo women have turned their experiences into something to benefit others. They coauthored a book, *Home Team*, about the experience, and they speak frequently to cancer victims and their families about learning to cope with the illness, their fears, and the uncertainty of their lives. Several years ago, the family established a scholarship for needy students at UConn's Allied Health School as another contribution to promoting health.

■ ■ ■

In some ways Kara Wolters, a 6'7" center at Connecticut in the mid-1990s, has had two family tragedies to deal with: the death of

Standing Tall

Rebecca Lobo's UConn Statistics

Games played: 126
Field goals: 837
Field goal average: 49.8 percent
3-point field goals: 58
3-point field-goal average: 33.9 percent
Free throws: 401
Free throw average: 69.5 percent
Rebounds: 1,268
Rebound average: 10.1
Assists: 260
Turnovers: 351
Steals: 130
Blocks: 396
Points: 2,133
Points per game: 16.9

Kara Wolters's UConn Statistics

Games played: 137
Field goals: 947
Field goal average: 62.8 percent
Free throws: 247
Free throw average: 58.4 percent
Rebounds: 927
Rebound average: 6.8
Assists: 130
Turnovers: 295
Steals: 51
Blocks: 370
Points: 2,141
Points per game: 15.6

her mother from a painful, aggressive cancer when she was fifty-seven, and her older sister Katie's debilitating brain tumor, for which she requires twenty-four-hour care.

Through the four long snowy winters of Wolters's career at UConn, Willie and Florence Wolters would pack up Katie in her wheelchair and head an hour south to Storrs from their home in Holliston, Massachusetts, to watch their daughter grow into one of the dominant centers in the women's game. It was to be the last time Florence Wolters would see her daughter play on a regular basis, because after graduation Kara left the area to play for a number of WNBA teams as well as abroad.

Florence Wolters died at Mass General Hospital on August 19, 2002. She was buried on her birthday—Kara brought a cake to the cemetery. Wolters had always looked up to Lobo but always felt she was in her shadow. Even in the area of illness, she felt Rebecca "lucked out: Rebecca's mom beat it and thank God her mother lived, but my mom didn't," Wolters said. One of her most cherished possessions from her college days is a picture of the Lobos and the Wolters at a game together, four stately parents basking in the glow of their daughters' accomplishments.

In other significant ways, the two players differed. Unlike Lobo, Wolters struggled with her height as well as her weight as she was growing up and got upset when kids called her "moose" or "freak" or other cruel names. "I was very sensitive . . . I just wanted to be loved and accepted," she said. Through these painful years, until she discovered that being tall could make her special, Florence Wolters, who was 6 feet herself, stood behind her daughter, reminding her to be proud of her height. "Sometimes I'd go to the school nurse because I was so hurt and my

At 6'7" Kara Wolters was one of the most dominating centers in the game. *University of Connecticut Division of Athletics* mom would come and pick me up from school. She would tell me, 'Don't worry about what those stupid kids call you.'"

Although her father's influence on his daughter's skills and goals was unmistakable (he set rebounding and field-goal records at Boston College in the mid-1960s), her mother was an integral part of her basketball life. In fact, during her own playing days at Wellesley (Massachusetts) High School, Florence Wolters set a single-game scoring record of 50 points. "She loved Emeka Okafor," Wolters said, referring to Connecticut's All-America center. "She used to say I block shots like I'm saluting Hitler when I should be doing it like Okafor—straight up. She was a huge part of my basketball support. I'm just grateful she lived to see me play."

The day Florence Wolters died, her family was gathered at her bedside. Kara had rushed back from South Korea where she was playing professionally after her family wrote that her mom had returned to the hospital because of a "groin pull." "I knew that wasn't true," Wolters said, suspecting her Dad was trying to protect her from the worst. "I said to myself, 'I'm coming home.' Something in my heart told me I had to get on a plane." This she did immediately, arriving at Mass General in time to meet with the physicians who told the family (including Florence) that at most she had two days to live.

That final day, a small miracle occurred. "God gave her the gift of one day and she felt great," Kara said. All of Florence Wolters's friends and family came to see her, they brought food— the atmosphere in the hospital room was celebratory and the patient, her sense of humor fully restored, felt like her old self for just that day. During the farewell party—for that's really what it was—Florence Wolters made sure she had a few serious moments with her daughter. "I'm not afraid to die," she told Kara and then gave her the best advice of her life—to hold on to her 6'1" boyfriend, Sean Drinan, even though Kara was bothered by the fact that he was 6 inches shorter than she was. A year ago they were married; in a video Drinan made for his new wife, he told her that her mother, Florence, was still there because "she left the best parts of her in you."

Several months before her mother died, Kara gave Florence a mother-daughter diary in case she felt like recording some thoughts. "She was in such pain, it was hard for her to write so I didn't push it," Kara said. In the rush of events that followed, she forgot about the diary. But then another small miracle occurred—on the anniversary of Florence's death, Kara discovered the book and noticed that her mother had written down some thoughts, among them a wish that her daughter's marriage would match the happiness she had experienced with Willie. It was a "gift to me," Kara said of the long-forgotten diary. "It felt like she was talking to me."

Through all the pain and grief of being teased as a kid, Kara Wolters, like Rebecca Lobo and Leigh Curl before her, finally realized that being tall is a special gift that can unlock the door to a passion. "Basketball was my drug," Wolters said. "My height had become a positive."

Like Lobo and Curl, Wolters has also reached out to help others heal. Several years ago she established the Kara Kares Foundation to raise funds for cancer research as well as for the Michael Carter Lisnow Center in Hopkinton, Massachusetts, where Katie is looked after most of her waking hours. Funds she raises at college and high-school basketball clinics, called Dream BIG (she's been called "Big Girl" for years), go to the foundation.

Wolters's father, Willie, meanwhile, has had to struggle to get over the loss of his wife of thirty-seven years and the increased burden of Katie's care. At first resentful, he has now discovered the full-time care has given him a focus and purpose. "He does this for my mom," Kara Wolters said of the deathbed promise he made to watch over Katie.

■　■　■

All three of these players—Leigh Curl, Rebecca Lobo, and Kara Wolters—survived some of life's biggest tests. The support of their mothers, the bonds they established with them living and dead, and this drug called basketball saw them through.

Diana Taurasi: The Greatest Player Ever

When Diana Taurasi came east from California for her visit at the University of Connecticut in the fall of 1999, reporters were more interested in her reaction to New England weather than her choice of college. Repeatedly she was asked two questions: Was she willing to go 3,000 miles from home? And was she concerned about the Connecticut snow?

To the first she was careful, although one got the distinct impression that distance was no object to her. Was leaving home an issue? "Sure," she replied, "but I have to do what's right for me." To the second she replied in that snappy manner that was to become her trademark: "They sell coats here, don't they?"

She was accompanied on that trip by her mother, Lily, like Diana, a woman with a great wit although she never laughed at the thought of her daughter moving so far from home. But Lily Taurasi got the most out of the trip to Connecticut. She missed the first half of the annual Supershow, which introduces the team to its fans, because she was playing the slot machines at one of Connecticut's casinos, an hour from Storrs.

Despite the pull of the slot machines, Lily Taurasi would have preferred Diana play at UCLA, where she would be an hour away from her home in Chino, California, a community of 67,000 east of Los Angeles. In fact the sport of basketball itself at one time presented problems for Lily Taurasi. With an Italian father (Mario) and Argentinian mother, soccer was the preferred sport for the athletic youngster. "We play soccer . . . this (basketball) is just for fun," Lily Taurasi once told Diana's AAU coach Lou Zilchers. She clung to that hope for just a couple of years as Diana was growing up, until friends and coaches began to tell her how gifted the girl was in basketball. She also displayed a talent for softball, in one game hitting a ball so hard her teammates in the field had to duck or lose their heads. "Mommy, I just do my best," Diana replied when her mother inquired about the incident.

Zilchers realized Taurasi was special the first time he saw her, during a recruiting session for an AAU team he was organizing in

Southern California. "She caught my eye immediately," he was to recall later. "Her feet were so quick compared to other kids. I said to myself, 'If this isn't the best player for her age group I've ever seen, then I don't know very much about basketball.'" Taurasi had a superlative for Zilchers as well when she whispered to another girl "We may not have the smartest coaches, but we have the fattest," referring to Zilchers and an assistant, both of whom were well over 6'5" and 300 pounds.

By the time she was ready for college, Taurasi had become what University of Connecticut coach Geno Auriemma calls a "recruiting legend." But if he was going to land her, he had some work to do. "The first time I met that man, I didn't like him," recalls Lily Taurasi. "He was going to take away my heart." The Italian-born coach went at it, speaking Italian to Mario, bringing them a bottle of wine that had their last name on the label, and finally, asking the parents the one important question: Do you want your daughter to be happy playing for a national championship team or staying home and never knowing that thrill? The answer was obvious.

More than any other player, Auriemma was determined not to let this one get away. He knew he was seeing a potential for greatness, and when he dared to entertain the notion of her playing for someone else, it was unbearable to contemplate. When she finally committed to Connecticut (during the early signing period in November 1999), he breathed a deep sigh of relief. "It was a great feeling to know that at least for the next four years, we had something that no one else did. A player like this only comes along once in a generation."

Taurasi's four years at UConn were a study in the development of a complete player. A strong-willed practical joker, she often ignored her coach, had bad practice habits, and laughed things off too easily, perhaps a defense against the expectations. But by the end of their association, a hug, in which she literally swept the coach, 2 inches shorter, off his feet at the last home game her senior year, spoke volumes of what had transpired during that sometimes rocky era.

Her career began on the Gampel Pavilion bench in the fall of 2000 when she averaged 10.6 points a game. Midway through the season she was starting. Even in her first year, she made it clear she was a big-game player, scoring 41 points in the two-game NCAA East Regional for which she was named most outstanding player, despite the plethora of blue chippers, most on her own team, that also had strong tournaments. The high point of her first regular season was when she scored 24 points at Tennessee. Against NC State in the NCAA regionals, she did it again and had 17 points against Louisiana Tech in the Final Eight. A week earlier she had had 53 points in three games in the Big East tournament and became the first rookie ever to be named the most outstanding player. When she shot 1 of 15 against Notre Dame in UConn's losing 2001 NCAA semifinal effort, she was distraught on the bench but when questioned about it later said it happens and it was time to move on. What she didn't do was blame it on anyone else. "As a freshman I started changing," she said once while looking back on her early college career. "I thought about being more of a team player—I always wanted to be that way." At Don Lugo High School, where she scored more than 3,000 points; she was the best player in California, but that wasn't enough to lead to any statewide championships; the value of teamwork had been driven home.

Diana Taurasi (left) hugs Tennessee's
Ashley Robinson following an NCAA game.
University of Connecticut Division of Athletics

In her sophomore season, she was a key part of the 39–0 team and finished second on the team in scoring (14.6 points a game). She had a lot of competition from her senior teammates, but even they recognized that the younger player could get the job done in the clutch. In five of six NCAA games that season, she averaged double figures and well over thirty-five minutes in each. She also was a first-team Kodak All-American, an honor she would earn twice more.

Taurasi's best year by far was her junior season when she led a team, decimated by the loss of two All-Americans, to a 37–1 record and the Huskies' second straight national championship. That season she averaged 17.9 points a game (54 points in the Final Four alone) and 4.8 assists. Connecticut had lost an average of 52 points and 25 rebounds a game with the graduation of four of its top players (Sue Bird, Tamika Williams, Asjha Jones, and Swin Cash), and it fell to Taurasi to fill in the gap. The biggest loss, however, was in leadership. Taurasi had always been vocal on the court—it's her nature to push and prod—but as long as the upperclassmen were around, she had to control herself. Once Bird and Cash were gone, her natural tendencies to get the most out of the players around her were unleashed. "She wasn't a leader as a freshman but she was the lady in waiting, ready to take the reins as soon as she needed to," Auriemma said. "She also had players like Shea Ralph to keep her in line."

Ironically, her senior year, when she should have had the basketball world by the tail, was her most difficult. Plagued by nagging injuries, usually double- and triple-teamed throughout a game (with or without the ball), and worn down mentally by the weight of the team on her shoulders, she fell into a mini–shooting slump midway through the year when she scored in single digits

The Day the Cheering Stopped

In Diana Taurasi's case, art imitates life. Taurasi was the subject of an oil painting by famed *Sports Illustrated* cover artist Donald Moss (a Farmington, Connecticut, resident and a UConn women's fan) in which the player, described by the artist as "rising like a phoenix," is shown getting off a shot while a small army of West Virginia defenders try unsuccessfully to stop her. It is, coach Geno Auriemma says, a perfect depiction of her toughness of being able to score with a lot of people around her. In the background of the painting, called *Diana Taurasi: All-American,* are impressionistic circles to represent the cheering fans, although on canvas they are paralyzed in silence. Taurasi's face is gripped in intensity; her legendary bun slightly disheveled at the back of her head.

The painting hangs in the Auriemma Family Reading Room of UConn's Homer Babbidge Jr. Library, a room partially paid for by funds from the coach and his wife, Kathy, to encourage students to take their education seriously. "This is the longest Diana has ever been in the library," Auriemma cracked at the official unveiling of the portrait. Moss, whose *SI* covers included paintings of Babe Ruth, Ted Williams, Robert Clemente, and countless other sports legends, had never painted a female athlete, but was "drawn" to the UConn women and especially Taurasi through watching the games on television. He had never attended a game, but tickets from the coach may have been his just reward for his generosity.

for several games. She talked with Auriemma about having fun on the court again, and the "fun" returned just in time for an important January 19 game in Hartford against Rutgers, a detested opponent, when she went off for 27 points. "I felt the last couple of games, everything was dragging along instead of being fun," she said of a pair of subpar performances. "[Tonight] was more fun— getting rebounds [4], making shots, getting loose balls [3 steals], just being aggressive. Hopefully that stretch was my lowest point. Now the minute I see it start to slide, I can get it back. The only way the team is good is if everyone takes it upon themselves from here on out."

Auriemma constantly tried to ease the burden on his star, reminding her that she should just worry about herself "and the rest will take care of itself." He had expected the pressure and the slump in her junior year. In fact he told her at the end of her sophomore year when the team lost so many good players that if she could get through her third year, "your senior year will be the greatest anyone ever had. It turns out this is last year," he said as she struggled in her final season. "She's not out here to prove she's the best player in the country. She's already that," he said. "Now she's just trying to make the rest of the team better," which in the end she did, leading them to their third straight national championship. In the Final Four, against Minnesota and Tennessee, she scored a total of 35 points.

After a tumultuous four years in which they frequently disagreed, some balance set into the relationship between coach and player, who shared an abundant supply of self-confidence, stubbornness, and belief that there wasn't much they couldn't accomplish if they set their minds to it. Auriemma had learned early on that Taurasi could be the master of manipulation. Her flip, niggling attitude prompted him to dub her the Eddie Haskell of Women's Basketball, but this was all surface stuff to tweak the media. When it counted, they saw eye to eye. Once, in commenting on their relationship, Auriemma made the observation that really mattered. "We understand each other so well. We know each others' strengths and each others' weaknesses. So everyone lives happily ever after."

Taurasi's desire to make her team better is perhaps most obvious in her success at becoming Connecticut's career assist leader, surpassing Jen Rizzotti (1992–96) with 648. "Personally the assist record means a lot. I love to pass," she said at the time. She also surpassed Wendy Davis's three-point record, with 318, another milestone she was typically cavalier about. "I just have a good time at it," she said once about her uncanny shooting abilities. And through the years her defense improved as well. "Every game we play, Dee gets the best guard," Auriemma said once during her senior year. "In her freshman year, she was guarding the ball rack." In her four years she averaged 4.5 assists a game, which would be expected of a great guard, but the remarkable thing about her defense is that at 6' she was fearless about going inside and usually led the team in blocked shots and was among the top three rebounders most seasons. In all, she had 147 blocks in four years, enough to make her the sixth best overall in team history. Her name stands out on a list of former players, easily well over 6 feet, who were used to playing in the post and typically towered over their opponents: 6'3" Rebecca Lobo, 6'7" Kara Wolters, 6'4" Kelly Schumacher.

When she finally finished her eligibility, the better coaches in the country breathed a sigh of relief. The next year, the team struggled. Despite their preseason assurances that someone else

Duking It Out

Diana Taurasi, one of two UConn three-time All-Americans (Svetlana Abrosimova, 1999–2001, is the other), was the consensus national player of the year in 2003–04, her junior year, capturing the Naismith, Wade, Honda, AP, and U.S. Basketball Writers Association trophies. Her senior year, however, bothered by injuries and the need to carry the team on her back for the second straight season, Taurasi struggled and took home only the Naismith and Honda Women's Basketball Player of the Year awards at the end of the season. Her chief rival was always Alana Beard, Duke's All-America guard who would have been all-world, herself, most of her career, if it hadn't been for UConn's number three. Beard came up empty her junior year because of Taurasi's glittering numbers, but in her senior year she made some headway, taking home the AP, Wade, and writers' association trophies. Yet in her four years, she never led her team to a national championship, while Taurasi won three straight.

The two games Connecticut and Duke played against each other when Taurasi and Beard were in school (they split them) brought out the best in both athletes. On February 1, 2003, Connecticut defeated Duke 77–65 in Durham; Beard had 26 points—the rest of her team was pitiful from the floor—and Taurasi, 17. Eleven months later, when Duke beat Connecticut in Hartford on a last-second three-pointer by sub Jessica Foley, Beard had 21 points and Taurasi, 16. Off the court, they were cordial. Even when backed into a corner by the media trying to stir things up before each of the two games, the two women took the high road and refused to trash each other. On the court they were like the Yankees and the Red Sox. Each expressed respect for her rival and left it at that. Their talking, they implied, would be done on the hardwood.

would fill the void, the Huskies finished the 2004–05 season 25–8 and were eliminated in the round of sixteen in the NCAA tournament, the earliest exit since 1999. Taurasi's points and ball handling were missing, but those are entities that can be replaced. The lack of leadership, the swagger, the attitude—those were the missing ingredients that mattered. "They're definitely a different team without her," said Notre Dame coach Muffett McGraw. She was never that devastating against the Irish as she was, say, when Connecticut played Tennessee, but the intangibles made the difference. "She was a great leader who inspired the rest of her team," McGraw said. "That attitude—you're not going to beat us—that's what's missing. The leadership, the confidence she inspired, you can't replace that."

Rutgers coach C. Vivian Stringer also noticed the difference, pointing out that Connecticut missed Taurasi especially in important Big East games. And Tennessee's Pat Summitt used to ask regularly, "Is that girl ever going to graduate?" Taurasi averaged more than 21 points in eight games against the Lady Vols (UConn was 7–1), including a 32-point performance her sophomore year that stood as her career high until she scored 35 in an NCAA early-round tournament game in March 2003. For sheer drama her most spectacular baskets against Tennessee came during a regular season game at the Hartford Civic Center in her junior year when she made a 45-foot shot from beyond half court to end the first half and then a three-point shot at the buzzer to give her team an overtime win.

Auriemma, who repeatedly referred to Taurasi as "the best women's basketball player in the country" as if it's all one word, used to compare her to guard Jennifer Rizzotti, one of his favorite players of all time. Taurasi had more natural abilities and "flash

Diana Taurasi waves the net after UConn won the NCAA East regional in 2004.
Willimantic Chronicle/Jared Ramsdell

and dash" than Rizzotti, the blue-collar player for whom a behind-the-back pass would be rare, contrasted with Taurasi, who thrived on the sneaky pass to a post player. She also drew far more defensive pressure than Rizzotti, Auriemma pointed out, forcing her to make quicker decisions. Auriemma also liked to note that Rizzotti and Taurasi had similar careers: near perfect junior years, in which they both led their teams to national championships, but struggles in their senior years to repeat as national champions.

Taurasi was back in Storrs for the bulk of the 2004–05 season, taking courses toward a degree in sociology, an education cut short by years of full-time basketball and the need to join her WNBA team, the Phoenix Mercury, before the spring 2004 semester ended. Once back in Storrs in January, she practiced with her old team but remained focused on the immediate goal of finishing her education and moving on. "You have to think in terms of balance . . . it's their team not mine. I try to help them out, but they have seniors who know what to do for the team."

She said she missed college because of the friendships she had made but knew it was time to leave it behind. "If you come here for four years, you should be prepared enough to move on. I was sad but sometimes it's time for a change. That's what the process is . . . four years." When she practiced with the team, sometimes it was her against the lot of them, putting on a clinic of shooting or stealing the ball while they stood around helplessly. Occasionally, and only occasionally, she got involved in off-the-court matters. When a freshman guard giggled at the fact that she was shooting only 20 percent from the three-point line, Taurasi practically grabbed her around the neck, telling her it was a serious matter. "The laughter was embarrassing," she said

Rewriting the Record Books

Among Diana Taurasi's achievements:

Two-time Naismith National Player of the Year (2003, 2004)

Three-time Kodak All-American (2002–04)

Two-time AP first-team All-American

First player in UConn history to achieve 2,000 points, 600 assists, 600 rebounds

Third all-time UConn scoring list (2,156 points) behind Nykesha Sales (2,178) and Kerry Bascom (2,177)

First, three-point field goals made (318)

First, career assists (648)

Third, career field goal percentage (81.5 percent)

Sixth, career blocks (147)

later. "You can't do that in front of the seniors. It's not funny." During her first few years at Connecticut, she was usually the person cracking jokes or making light of situations, prompting the then upperclassmen to teach her lessons about respect and decorum. Now fully mature with all of that knowledge under her belt, she had earned the right to pass it on herself.

Although she knew her talents were extraordinary, she also learned to handle the fame and notoriety that came with them with maturity and humility. Once when someone labeled her the best player of her generation, she pointed out that "every generation has its great players," mentioning Cheryl Miller and Lisa Leslie, two of her own Southern California role models. The players of the twenty-first century now have another "best player of her generation" (some would say ever) to point to, and the state of Connecticut was fortunate to host her for four years. "I don't think anyone could have asked for any more out of a career," she said toward the end of her senior year. But then she added, "This is what I knew was going to happen. That's why I came: I had confidence in the people here, in the people they drew here, and in myself."

If Lily Taurasi had any doubts about her daughter's decision so many years ago, they were laid to rest senior night when the usually enthusiastic crowd gave her the longest standing ovation in UConn women's basketball history. And Lily and Mario were with her at center court to hear the roar.

Getting a Life

Their star-studded success as players still shines throughout the women's basketball world through a galaxy of former UConn athletes now coaching at other universities. Some are on the lowest rung of the ladder, in the first few years as assistants; others are already head coaches, their reputations and visions trusted by athletic directors to run the show.

None of these former players is attached to programs with the brilliance of their alma mater, but if they choose to, most will move up in the ranks, bringing with them the tradition of winning, discipline, and hard work that was drilled into them by their former coach, Geno Auriemma.

In a profession hungry for successful female role models, Jen Rizzotti, Carla Berube, Wendy Davis, and Paige Sauer (as of 2004, eleven former players are coaching basketball) are a welcome departure from more traditional coaches, male and female, who had difficulty spurring young women to join them in the profession.

These former players had different reasons for becoming coaches. Some tried other things first; others went right from the court to the bench, but all share two things: Each said she missed having basketball in her life, and each said she wanted to give something back to the game that had given her so much.

Among those who waited a few years after graduating before becoming a coach is Jen Rizzotti, whose post as head coach at the Division I University of Hartford is perhaps more prestigious and carries more responsibility than those of her UConn colleagues.

"I didn't have any idea that I was going to get into coaching, but now that I'm into it, it was meant to be my profession," said Rizzotti, whose pluck symbolizes UConn basketball.

A straight-A biology major, Rizzotti entered the postcollege ranks as a player with the New England Blizzard in the now defunct American Basketball League. When the ABL folded in 1999, the point guard, who led Connecticut to an NCAA national championship and national runner-up, played with a few WNBA teams before being hired in September 1999, at Hartford by athletic director Pat Meiser-McKnett, once UConn women's athletic administrator who oversaw the hiring of Geno Auriemma in 1985. A sudden resignation by a former head coach left Meiser-McKnett in a rush to find a replacement. Rizzotti, a Connecticut native who lived in nearby Glastonbury, had just completed her second WNBA season with the Houston Comets. Since she wasn't ready to give up her pro career, she would only accept the job on an interim basis, but Meiser-McKnett had another agenda.

"I thought 'I know this young lady—if I can just get the hook in her, she'll love the game,'" Meiser-McKnett said. "She already coaches from the point guard position. Then the first day I saw her on the floor, I said 'It's over.'" Rizzotti's leadership and enthusiasm made her a natural for the job, but she was still playing with the WNBA Cleveland Rockers and had no intention of giving that up. Although the pro and college seasons do not overlap, there was still the issue of off-season recruiting and administrative work that comes with the job. Meiser-McKnett was resolute and, through some negotiations with the NCAA, figured out a way Rizzotti could play and coach at the same time, and she was named permanent coach the following year. Finally, in 2002 she ended her playing career. The dual responsibilities apparently didn't affect her ability as a coach because in the 2001–02 season, she led the Hawks to a record sixteen wins as well as an America East Conference championship and first-ever NCAA appearance.

And now? "She's a remarkable young woman . . . she can stand in front of the General Assembly and take it over, or sit with a kid who is crying . . ." Meiser-McKnett said of Rizzotti's skills and talent as a communicator.

Since she's been at Hartford, she's been offered coaching jobs at more prestigious Division I schools in New England, but she's satisfied to stay in her home state, where she was raised in New Fairfield, a small community near Danbury. In fact there are those who think somewhere down the line Jen Rizzotti will be coaching at her alma mater. But she still has a way to go.

For now she's content at Hartford, in a job that, she says, "kind of grew on me." She remains firmly entrenched in the Connecticut sports scene, making television ads for a prominent Hartford-area Honda dealer, appearing as a speaker at fund-raising and other events, and, in general, maintaining the popularity and respect of state sports fans that began when she was a player.

She has just completed her sixth year with a 92–85 record as head coach at Hartford, a modest suburban campus about forty minutes from Storrs — so close, in fact, that at least once a season, she brings some members of her team to watch how Auriemma runs a practice. "I like for the players I bring to see how hard they work and how demanding he is," she said.

In December 2004 UConn and Hartford played their first game against each other, a highly anticipated matchup in the Hartford Civic Center that drew a capacity crowd of more than 16,000. UConn won but Hartford was prepared and played such stinging defense on the Huskies that the game was closer than expected.

Because Hartford plays in a minor conference, it's not likely to get an NCAA bid unless it wins the league tournament, which it did in 2005. So Rizzotti has had to scale back her expectations and work with what she has, but it would be foolish to think she has compromised her standards.

"I've learned to be just as picky and just as much a perfectionist as he is," she said, referring to Auriemma. And the players learn this, too. "We are going to do things as perfectly as we can . . . every drill. I demand that of my players. The closer to perfection (in practices), the better they'll be in games."

Rizzotti continues: "I believe that if you make your practices harder than any game, if you put your kids in situations more

difficult than in any game, then they'll be ready for anything."
This is Auriemma talking—Auriemma who says a thousand
times a season that he usually can tell how well his team will play
based on the practices leading up to a game. Auriemma who
believes that intrasquad scrimmages should be harder for his
players than the games.

Rizzotti sees her role as a benevolent adversary to her players—
a posture Geno Auriemma also adopts. "If I'm their biggest adversary, then I'm doing the right job," she said. "He makes himself
their biggest enemy in practice. So do I . . . I want to create
competitiveness and for them to feel every possession matters."

As complete a player as she was, Rizzotti, like all of
Auriemma's athletes, frequently felt the sting of his anger through
a gesture or a shout during practices if she failed to go hard or
made a bad decision or missed a defensive assignment. It is this
adversarial nature that she refers to when speaking of being the
enemy on weekday afternoons as her team prepares for games.

The need to yell at players has discouraged some former
UConn players from entering the coaching ranks. Rebecca Lobo,
one of the best to wear the blue and white, said she never consid-
ered coaching for a moment. "I'm just not built for it. I can't see
myself yelling at kids all day . . . I have no interest in that at all,"
said Lobo, who took the art of being thoughtful and responsive to
reporters and her teammates to a new level from 1991 to 1995
when she broke records at UConn. Instead of coaching, she stays
close to the game as a television analyst for the WNBA, a profession that suits the well-spoken intelligent woman.

Lobo's former teammate, Carla Berube, came to her
coaching career after several years without basketball. In 2002 she
was hired as head coach at Tufts University, a small, liberal arts

college in the Boston suburb of Medford, Massachusetts, as difficult to get into as any of the better-known Ivy League universities.

Berube tried plenty of other things first. She, too, played with the New England Blizzard until the ABL folded, and then she moved to California where she held a number of odd jobs. "I thought about coaching while I was in college," she said, "but after the ABL went under, I just wanted to get away from basketball completely for a while." When she found herself missing the sport, the Oxford, Massachusetts, native contacted Auriemma and some UConn assistant coaches to see if they knew of any assistant openings on the East Coast. "I started to feel I wanted to give something back to the game," she said.

Sure enough, Providence College, Connecticut's most fierce Big East rival in the 1980s, had an opening, so Berube joined that staff as an assistant. For two years she learned the trade and found out that coaching is more than just going to practice. "I learned a lot of behind the scenes stuff that you never think of as a player," she said, "such as how to construct a team, how to design practices, how to make it all work." She was also schooled on scouting opponents, making sure players maintain their academic records—off the court stuff that all programs must take into account, successful or not. Providence hasn't been successful in years—in the two years Berube was an assistant under Jim Jabir (since fired), the team went 10–21 and one year failed to qualify for the Big East tournament.

After two years at PC, Tufts called and she jumped at the opportunity to be a head coach at a school that placed a high priority on academics. "I felt this was really the kind of job I wanted," she said. "It's not a business . . . The people I am coaching are playing with me because they love the game, not because they have a scholarship." This level of commitment appealed to her as did the assurance that when it came to recruiting players, the academic reputation of the school would help sell the basketball program. Although the pool of candidates is smaller for her than other Division III schools because of the stiff scholastic requirements, there are plenty of talented, intelligent young women who are seeking a Tufts education and want to play competitive basketball as well.

Sometimes they're too intelligent for their own good. "They need to know answers for everything," Berube said. "Sometimes I have to tell them 'just play basketball . . . stop analyzing everything.'"

But they must be doing something right . . . or at least their coach is. Since she arrived, Berube has turned the program around with four straight winning seasons and an overall record of 49–23. The team is among the leaders in the New England Small College Athletic Conference. "I brought a passion for the sport and pushed them to their limits," she says.

Sound familiar? "These are all the things I learned from UConn. I know what it takes to get there," Berube said. Like Rizzotti, Berube occasionally brings her players to UConn practices to pick up pointers and to show them how hard they have to work to be competitive. She runs many of the same drills she learned in college and makes sure every practice covers every aspect of the game. Her connection with UConn has helped her recruit players, some of whom have been lifelong fans. "I have one player from Connecticut who knew exactly who I was and what I did. She always wears a UConn championship T-shirt to practice," Berube said.

And for Carla Berube, who was first off the bench at UConn, coaching at a Division III school offers another advantage: a life.

"It's great here because it's not basketball all the time like it is at Division I," she said. "I get to be involved with other things going on . . . I teach Pilates and a sports conditioning class, I have to be at other athletic events on campus, I work with other coaches. It's nice to have other interests," she said.

Having a life is also important to Wendy Davis. UConn's career three-point leader (279 in 127 games) until Diana Taurasi broke that record in 2004 (318 in 144 games), Davis always gave her studies and her outside life as much attention as she could while playing at Connecticut in 1989–92. A number of regional and national organizations named her to their academic All-America teams, and when she graduated she received an NCAA postgraduate scholarship, which she used to get her master's in education at UConn while she was a student-coach for a year. For most of her life, Davis had her hopes set on a teaching career, which she pursued for a while back in tiny Birdsboro, Pennsylvania, where she is from. She soon realized that teaching wasn't her life's desire after all, although she still wasn't ready to go back to basketball. "I didn't miss basketball the first couple of years I was out," she said. "I truly needed a break from it—I didn't want to talk about it, I didn't want to look at a ball, and I certainly didn't want to play it."

Finally, though, she changed her mind and returned to Connecticut to try out for the Blizzard (she was the last cut) and then worked in a number of jobs, not the least among them was climbing telephone poles hundreds of feet in the air to repair wires. "I felt I needed to be outside. I saw this and went for it," she said of the job that for one mildly afraid of heights was more risky than any of the three-point baskets she took while a player.

Filling Out the Ranks

Here are some other former UConn women's basketball players who are in either coaching or athletic administration:

Kathy Bantley (1986–90): Head women's basketball coach, Elms College.

Jamelle Elliott (1993–96): assistant women's basketball coach, University of Connecticut

Debbie (Baer) Fiske (1988–92): assistant athletic director, head coach, women's basketball, St. Joseph's College, West Hartford, Connecticut

Courtney Gaine (1996–2000): sports nutritionist for UConn student athletes

Stacy Hansmeyer (1996–2000): assistant women's basketball coach, University of Oklahoma

Kris Lamb (1986–90): assistant women's basketball coach, University of Hartford

Ellen Mahoney (1968–72): assistant softball coach, University of Connecticut

Karen Mullins (1975–79): head softball coach, University of Connecticut

Shea Ralph (1997–2001): assistant women's basketball coach, University of Pittsburgh

Tamika Williams (1998–2002): assistant women's basketball coach, Ohio State University

The following fall, Davis decided she could make a difference in young players' lives and in 1999 became the head coach at Western New England College in Springfield, Massachusetts. In six years she accumulated a 105-55 record. (She turned down an assistant coaching position at Yale for the WNEC job because, after talking with some teammates, she decided at this stage in her career Division III was the right fit.)

Davis prefers Division III because, she says, "It's just a different animal as far as time commitment, the type of student-athlete you get, all kinds of things. These kids play because they want to, not because they're being paid to play," she said echoing Berube's sentiments about Tufts athletes. Davis's concern with being well-rounded herself was transferred to her athletes, whom she encouraged to get involved in as many campus activities as they had time for. "There are so many things they can do, whereas at Division I it's basketball, school, and that's it. When I was in college, all I focused on was basketball. I had no social life outside of the team." Davis also said she could establish a more well-rounded relationship with her players. "I have a chance to get to know them at a different level . . . if I can't joke around with them and have fun, they can just quit because I'm not paying them a dime."

In the summer of 2005, Davis moved on in the Division III ranks accepting a position as head coach of women's basketball at Trinity College in Hartford, a school that prides itself on its scholarship and activities. She said she made the move from one Division III school to another, "because that's the level I love and that's the level I will always stay at."

However, Trinity offered some pluses she wasn't necessarily getting before. "It is moving forward," she said. "Trinity College is a nationally known college academically and athletically, and the New England Small College Athletic Conference is one of the best in the country. This is definitely a positive thing for me," she said.

Davis also said it will be great being back in Connecticut . . . no doubt she'll face another former UConn player since Wesleyan (where Berube coaches) is one of Trinity's major rivals.

At schools like Trinity and Western New England, basketball is not a twelve-month-a-year concern. When she was in Massachusetts, Davis called her team together two weeks prior to the season for conditioning, but after the season she said she didn't require anything at all. "At UConn it was two weeks off and then back at it. If my kids are in the gym playing pickup, it's because they want to, not because the coaches require it."

In fact, at Western New England, the basketball scene was so laid-back during the summer that Davis even found time for another job working at a nearby Costco. "I loved it. Instead of being a leader, I was a follower . . . just a regular person. It was a break from all this nonsense."

"This nonsense" enriched her life, perhaps more as a coach than it did as a player. "My biggest hope is that I not only make them better basketball players but better human beings," she said of her team. At Western New England, one way she incorporated that goal into her basketball routine was to allow her players to take part in collegewide "make a difference" days, for example, where everyone did some kind of community service. In effect, she said to them, "You'd better be a good human being, or I don't want you on my team." She expects to set the same standards at Trinity College.

Like others who have followed in Auriemma's professional footsteps, Davis credited him with everything she did as a coach at

Western New England. When she was there she said, "My practices are run similar to his, we still run plays that I ran. All our drills, all our plays are what I did at UConn–double screens at the foul line for the three-point shooter [like they used to run for her], Chicago," she said, referring to Auriemma's Chicago Bulls-like motion offense with its multipass, find-the-open-man rules. When she took her kids to UConn for a practice, which she did early in the fall, they'd say, "Hey, Coach, we do that drill; hey, Coach, we run that play." "That was a fun time for us," Davis said. After practice they'd go to Willington Pizza, a popular local Italian restaurant where for years a brownie-and-ice-cream concoction bore the name "The Kara Wolters" for the popular former UConn player.

Davis said Auriemma has influenced her so immensely that she wrote him a two-page letter "just letting him know how much I appreciate everything he has done for me in my life and professional life. His work ethic, from being tough on someone, yet still showing you care for them as a person . . . the little things . . . I tell my kids if someone dives on the floor for the ball, there better be four other people sprinting back to pick that kid up. Simple things like standing and clapping when your teammate comes out of the game," a UConn ritual usually led by the players who get the least amount of playing time.

Just like at UConn, practices at Western New England were noisy, and she expects the same at Trinity College. "My kids were never allowed to be silent. They were either clapping or encouraging each other."

Davis said parents of opposing team members have commented on the fact that their daughters' teams were quiet whereas her team was on its feet cheering. "When people noticed that, it made me feel good . . . I got that from Coach."

"Coach" likes to say that Davis is one of the few players he *didn't* have to yell at. She did everything right. But he yelled plenty at Paige Sauer and worse. In Sauer's senior year, a lack of speed and an injured ankle caused her to lose her starting job. These days, as an assistant to Fairfield University women's basketball coach Dianne Nolan, it's Sauer who has to break bad news to players, news she herself bore stoically in the interest of the team. After she was benched, Sauer turned her thoughts to one thing: winning a national championship, which Connecticut did in 2000. Paige Sauer played three minutes. "I had to put individual thoughts and feelings aside," she said.

After graduation in 2000, Sauer played in the WNBA (it was her misfortune — or good fortune — to be Lisa Leslie's backup in Los Angeles) and then went abroad for a few years where she had a successful pro career in South Korea, the Canary Islands, and Hungary among other countries. When she had gotten playing out of her system, she decided she missed Connecticut ("people there had been so good to me"), and so she moved to southern Connecticut, heard about the Fairfield opening, and was hired.

The experience has taught her among other things that most of the college basketball world is very different than that of the University of Connecticut. "What happens at UConn doesn't happen everywhere else, but when you're going through it for four years, you don't think about that," she said, referring to the packed arenas, the winning traditions, the level of athlete that plays there. "Coach demanded perfection," she said of Auriemma. "But he could because he had those athletes. Here I could never say to a kid 'Why can't you do that? We did that at Connecticut.' But although we can't expect kids to do certain things, we can expect effort. That's the biggest thing I learned from being at UConn. How hard you have to work."

She's also found out that coaching is a twenty-four-hour job—that there's always something that needs attending to. "I remember when I was at UConn, I'd say, 'Jamelle go home,' and she'd say, 'I can't. I have too much to do,'" Sauer said, referring to assistant coach Jamelle Elliott, a former Connecticut player, who stayed on as Auriemma's assistant after her playing career ended in 1996. "I found out that it's not what you see on the court—that so much goes on behind the scenes to make a team successful," Sauer said.

But despite the hard work, a losing season is a losing season. In just her first year at Fairfield, the Stags went 8–18, a humbling experience for a player whose teams lost only seven games in her four years at college. "It's hard being on the other end," she said. The next year they went 11–16 in the regular season, so things were starting to improve. She also has learned the difference between being a buyer in the recruiting market and a seller. When Sauer was in high school in Midwest City, Oklahoma, Tennessee and Connecticut engaged in a fierce recruiting war to land her. But now she's the one chasing the athletes, and it's a role she's not yet comfortable with. "The biggest change is going from a recruited student athlete to soliciting student athletes," she said. "It's a lot harder being the seller."

Still she has met with some success. In Sauer's first year on the job, Fairfield signed its top four recruits for the 2004–05 season— the first time Nolan had been that successful. Sauer is hopeful that success will carry over to the court, but she knows the pitfalls. "It's hard being on the other end," she said. "Once kids get on the court, you don't have that much control. I can't tell you how many times I wanted to put on a Fairfield uniform and play with them."

Since the former center is in charge of the post players, she regularly runs drills that she did at UConn, drills she learned from Auriemma, Elliott, and associate head coach Chris Dailey. "Coach is so knowledgeable about the game . . . he taught me so much I've taken with me, whether it's how to do a layup or how to run a zone defense."

Sauer aspires to be a head coach one day. She is working on her master's in psychology, a profession that also appeals to her, but since she took the job with Nolan, she says she can't imagine being "anywhere but on the court. It's like with Jamelle and CD [Dailey]—that's my life."

Nolan said Sauer has brought energy and personality to the job: "She's very knowledgeable and she's fun. That's a rare combination in coaching." But there are other, intangible qualities she brings to the sidelines, especially as a role model for the post players. "She's probably one of the few people who can carry their height the way she does," Nolan said of the 6'5" Sauer. "She's very gregarious and draws people in. They're almost in awe of her because of her presence." Nolan said people whisper, "How tall is she?" when she passes them in the hall, but it doesn't phase her. "Most people 6'5" try to be 6'4"; Paige tries to look 6'7"." She encourages her players to wear heels instead of flats, to stand up tall instead of hunching over, and, in general, to be proud of what the good Lord gave them.

Like the other Auriemma disciples, Sauer's tools are an outstanding work ethic, humility, and a desire to be competitive. "In today's day and age, it's too often instant gratification and shortcutting," Nolan said. "She says you don't win that way. If you have to run a mile, you run a mile."

Auriemma can claim every success known in his profession,

but when you ask him about the coaches he has spawned, he gets a satisfied smile on his face and jokes about how they all inherited a little piece of his temper. He also knows with these women, the game is in good hands. "They were all passionate about the game and they wanted to continue that down the road. I guess it says a little about what we do here and how we do it," he said once.

The women who lit up the scoreboard in Storrs, Connecticut, and throughout the country may still insist their players run the same mile they did. The qualities that drove them when they played college basketball will make them successful on their new campuses, and in the end, the sport of women's basketball will be the real winner.